Early Praise for *The Developer's Code*

This is the next *Pragmatic Programmer*—a guide for the beginner, a reminder for the expert, and a wonderful chunk of wisdom about the craft (and life) of a developer.
➤ **Derek Sivers, founder of CD Baby, sivers.org**

Ka Wai Cheung has written a book for professional developers seeking a code they can live by. This is not a book replete with conventional, find-it-in-any-blog ideas but a very powerful, focused approach to the craft and realities of professional programming.

If you are looking for a rehash of stale, sterile rules for programming, this is not the book for you. But if you are seeking a perspective on what creating software is, or if you want a set of guidelines laden by real-world experience, this is a book you need.
➤ **Bob Walsh, author and founder of 47 Hats**

Packed with delicious lessons yet consumable in bite (byte?) sized chunks —there's a lot to be learned in these pages. Take some time and learn from someone who's been there.
➤ **Adam Hoffman, senior development lead**

A great book filled with lots of hints, tips, and lessons learned in the fast-moving world of the modern-day programmer; a must-read for anyone working as, or with, a developer.
➤ **Caspar Dunant, Webfish**

The Developer's Code

What Real Programmers Do

Ka Wai Cheung

The Pragmatic Bookshelf

Dallas, Texas • Raleigh, North Carolina

Many of the designations used by manufacturers and sellers to distinguish their products are claimed as trademarks. Where those designations appear in this book, and The Pragmatic Programmers, LLC was aware of a trademark claim, the designations have been printed in initial capital letters or in all capitals. The Pragmatic Starter Kit, The Pragmatic Programmer, Pragmatic Programming, Pragmatic Bookshelf, PragProg and the linking *g* device are trademarks of The Pragmatic Programmers, LLC.

Every precaution was taken in the preparation of this book. However, the publisher assumes no responsibility for errors or omissions, or for damages that may result from the use of information (including program listings) contained herein.

Our Pragmatic courses, workshops, and other products can help you and your team create better software and have more fun. For more information, as well as the latest Pragmatic titles, please visit us at *http://pragprog.com*.

Cartoons courtesy of Mark Anderson, reproduced with permission of the artist. *http://www.andertoons.com*

The team that produced this book includes:

Brian P. Hogan (editor)
Kim Wimpsett (copyeditor)
David J Kelly (typesetter)
Janet Furlow (producer)
Juliet Benda (rights)
Ellie Callahan (support)

Printed in the United States of America.
ISBN-13: 978-1-934356-79-1
Printed on acid-free paper.
Book version: P1.0—February 2012

Contents

Acknowledgments

In the fall of 2010, with much of the original draft complete, I began pitching this book to several tech publishers. While I received some great feedback, I wasn't able to land a deal. The prevailing argument from most publishers was twofold: books like this typically don't sell, and in order to make it a worthwhile investment, I needed a bigger following.

Andy Hunt and Dave Thomas saw things differently. And so, first and foremost, I'd like to thank Andy and Dave for sharing my belief that this book has a place in our industry. I'm absolutely humbled to have it added to the great collection of works from the Pragmatic Bookshelf.

A book like this desperately needs a great editor—one who tells it like it is and sees the content from 1,000 feet above when the author is entangled in the weeds. I'd like to thank Brian P. Hogan for being a fantastic one throughout the entire process. This book is leagues ahead of where it initially was, in both its content and its approach.

A very special thanks to Mark Anderson of Andertoons.com. His creative cartoons—and wit—are strewn all over these pages. They provide a wonderful extra dose of levity and personality to the final product.

Thanks to Derek Sivers, Bob Walsh, Caspar Dunant, Colin Yates, Juho Vepsäläinen, Steve Cholerton, and Kim Shrier for generously donating their time to critically reviewing each and every chapter.

Much of the inspiration for this book came from the experiences I've had at We Are Mammoth, the web development shop I started with Craig Bryant in 2006. For the past five years, we've continually challenged ourselves, questioned the way we go about our work, and openly exposed our opinions to each other. Thanks to my team—Craig, Michael, Mustafa, Tom, Sam, Anthony, Jennifer, Grant, and Lindsay —for teaching me new lessons daily.

CHAPTER 1

Introduction

I've been had by code. Twice.

The very first time was when I took a programming class during my freshman year of college. It was a mandatory course for the curriculum I had decided to enroll in. It wasn't like what I had seen in so many movies during my childhood. I didn't type in a few simple commands, press ENTER, and watch a trash-can robot say "hello."

There wasn't even a trash-can robot in this class. Instead, it was about pointers, memory allocation, and object instantiation. I was too in the weeds to see what all of it meant. However, the evidence was overwhelmingly clear: programming was not for me.

I wanted to be an artist or perhaps a mathematician. I wanted to be both creative and exact—both right- and left-brained, as they say. Programming seemed to lean too far to the left, and no other career options I could think of let me play in both worlds simultaneously. I was lost.

Just a couple years later, the Internet boom changed the landscape of programming. Suddenly, it was real-world, it was approachable, and it had *a lot* to do with design. It valued both artistry and logic almost equally. For the first time, I really could foresee myself enjoying this work. I could now channel my passion for creativity and logic into web applications. So, I returned to programming, albeit with great apprehension.

Truth be told, I also came back to it for an entirely different reason. For that two-year hiatus, I studied many other subjects that seemed to have too many unanswered questions. Devising the Grand Unified Theory in particle physics or finding the largest prime number? Impossibly ambitious and daunting undertakings, for sure. They just weren't for me. In addition, that course on existentialism didn't clear things up either. As a young adult, I simply wanted *answers*, not more *questions*.

Programming. The very subject I had once eschewed was now my refuge. After all, computer science was man-made. All the answers had to be there. I yearned for a career where answer seekers like me could thrive, where you turned elixirs of code into always-happy customers, comrades, and clients. The rules were already written. We just had to build. All the obstacles existed solely in code, I thought.

In my second return to programming, I was duped again, because this was certainly far from the truth.

Who Is the 21st-Century Programmer?

As I would find out over the next fifteen years, programming isn't a job for the reclusive. It *certainly* is not about the über-nerd sitting in a dimly lit basement, sweating away for months on end, and then emerging with the final product in all its glory.

Today's applications are mainstream. We build for every user. Our clients may or may not have any idea about how we work. Our turnaround times are sometimes on the order of whirlwind weeks, not months or years. Burnout can come on suddenly; procrastination can be the path of least resistance. For us, the developers of today, building software involves *obstacles* that go far beyond what we encounter in our development environment.

One of my good friends jokes with me on a regular basis. "What exactly is it that *you do* for work?" She knows I'm a programmer but doesn't really know what that means. She questions me in that same sarcastic, probing way that Bob Slydell does as the office consultant in *Office Space*.

I tell her this: I am a nonaccredited, overly logical psychologist, therapist, mechanic, diplomat, businessman, and teacher working in an industry that is *still* defining itself each and every day.

That is as concise a definition I can give for the modern-day programmer.

Discovering the Lessons Firsthand

My name is Ka Wai Cheung. I'm a developer, designer, and founding partner at We Are Mammoth in Chicago.[1] We build applications for a variety of clients and create some of our own web-based software. You'll hear a bit more about those later.

This book is a collection of lessons, observations, and missteps I've gathered, firsthand, in our industry. For seasoned programmers, you might find some of my anecdotes similar to your own experiences. We can laugh, cheer, and cry through them together. For newbies beginning the journey, let this be a helping hand through your first few years in the industry.

In the last fifteen years, I've encountered myriad lessons. Here are just some of the topics we'll address in this book:

- Why many traditional development processes and role definitions in this industry are antiquated—and how to sniff them out

- Why saying "no" to the software pet project and open-ended timelines is essential to productivity

- How collaborative work environments can make us so much more productive—and how they can also make us so much less

- How to make code generation a natural part of the development process and how it benefits us in ways besides faster code output

- How to best work with clients who don't see eye-to-eye to us and how to handle angry customers who immediately dismiss new changes to our software

---

1. Our website is at http://www.wearemammoth.com, and our blog is at http://blog.wearemammoth.com.

- Why big raises and the old mantra "Employees are our greatest asset" don't equate to a better tech job

- How to recognize when software is becoming too complex for its own good

- How to become a better teacher so we can pay our knowledge forward to future generations of developers

This Book Is About Us

This is a book for developers of all kinds. However, it has little to do with code. It doesn't matter if you program in C# or Ruby or Python or PHP or Java or JavaScript or Action-Script. It doesn't matter whether you're working on databases, writing server-side code, or scripting the interface. This book is about everything that surrounds the professional developer beyond the bounds of markup and objects.

That doesn't mean we'll leave programming in the dust, though. There will be *some* talk about code. However, when we talk about code, we'll approach it in a less technical, far more holistic way. You won't see a laundry list of best practices or design patterns. Plenty of books do a great job of that, and we'll mention a few along the way.

This book is about what real, modern-day programmers do to flourish in our industry. Let's begin.

CHAPTER 2

Metaphor

A programmer *programs*. A designer *designs*. But what does that really mean? There are no reality television shows or Hollywood films that showcase how we really work. And before you say anything, no, *The Social Network* doesn't count as a representative look into our industry. So, when I'm asked what I do, I often resort to analogy. Our industry is chock-full of them. It's the way we describe our work to everyone else.

A chef doesn't have to come up with metaphors for cooking; a broth is too salty because you can taste it. A musician doesn't have to describe songs in some roundabout way; a melody is too cliché because you've heard the same rhythm before. People get it. They are self-describing forms of work. Pipe fitters and bricklayers have the job description succinctly written right in their names.

However, programming is different. The average person can't see what makes code elegant or unorganized. In addition, our industry is *very* new. While humans have been cooking, making music, and building for thousands of years, archaeologists have yet to discover those cave paintings of *Man at His Desk Typing*.

So, metaphor has to become our meta-language. Not only is it how we connect the uniqueness of programming to the general public, but it's often how we make decisions on how we approach our own software problems.

Follow Metaphors with Care

And this is where things get dangerous.

Sometimes the line between analogy and reality blurs. Metaphors can make us value things that aren't that important while undervaluing the things that are.

When we take these comparisons too far, we don't make our best decisions. Metaphor has a devilish way of blinding us to the truth. Our decisions might make perfect sense in the context of the metaphor, but when stripped down to just the business of building applications, we can easily be led astray. We sometimes rely on the perceived benefits of the metaphor too heavily rather than paying attention to the reality of the situation.

For instance, we often use traditional architecture as a metaphor for building software. After all, it's the origin of most of our organizational titles. That's why we call ourselves *software architects, information architects, senior developers, junior developers,* and *project managers.* That's why many of us still swear by wireframes, specifications, workflow diagrams, Gantt charts, and waterfall development. We've built a large portion of the software development process by piggybacking off of another industry.

While these concepts are essential in another medium and they have *some* merit in our world as well, they can just as easily imprison us. If we stop to think about why we approach a problem in a certain way, we might be able to trace its origins to following the metaphor of traditional architecture (or another metaphor) too closely.

So, how has metaphor hurt us? Let's look at a few examples where we've stretched a concept from real architecture into a less-than-ideal fit for software.

Plan Enough, Then Build

In traditional architecture, planning is essential. Certain things unequivocally have to happen before others. Studs go in before plumbing. Plumbing is installed before the walls. The walls have to be there before the paint. Undo, Cut, or Revert aren't viable options when building a skyscraper.

The software Undo is CTRL+Z. The software Cut is CTRL+X. The software Revert is a code rollback in source control.

"There's no Ctrl-X. That's what your scissors are for."

Without the luxury of these very simple yet powerful gestures, buildings require very detailed specifications. One foot short is the difference between a profitable piece of real estate and a catastrophic front-page headline.

Let's pretend we're traditional architects afforded all the shortcuts of software development. It would be a dream world. Materials would be infinitely available. We could build a life-size model of a building in a few weeks. We could stress test suspension bridges over and over again. If a bridge broke, who would care? We could instantaneously replicate ten new ones in a few minutes!

Of course, all of this is mere fantasy. So, writing specifications in excruciating detail makes the most sense when we've decided to build a skyscraper.

On the other hand, these *are* the luxuries of our industry. Software components don't need to wait on a shipment of letters and numbers from the local factory. We type, compile, test, and repeat. We can test code on the real product, not some model of the real product. We have the luxury of watching our suspension bridges break hundreds of times while in development, in all different places, under all different conditions, without the worry of wasting materials or putting people's lives in jeopardy. Working this way is completely feasible. When we finish software, the same application can be duplicated 1,000 times with negligible human effort.

When the developers of the Wynn Hotel in Las Vegas built a virtually identical twin hotel called the Encore in 2008, they didn't have the luxury of copying and pasting the first version into the vacant lot next door. They had to start with specs and planning just to build a nearly identical structure.

Even when software meant shipping code on a disk, planning extensively still made a lot of sense. Meanwhile, web-based software is a different game. Planning through very detailed specifications prior to writing a line of code still has merits, but it doesn't fully take advantage of the medium. We can release new builds daily or hourly or whenever we want, with very low overhead, from the comfort of our cushy Aeron chairs.

Fortunately, as an industry, we're starting to break through the metaphor. Agile development isn't revolutionary; it's just untying us from a metaphor that doesn't make as much sense today as it did in the past. That's not to say that traditional waterfall development is obsolete. It still has its merits on larger, more complex software projects. But following that metaphor without question might also blind us to an approach that better fits the medium we work in.

The "plan, plan, plan" metaphor overvalues the time we spend trying to get everything perfect and undervalues the time we could be spending writing the actual code.

Essay 3

Launch Is Just the First Release

Traditionally, we've approached a launch date as a mission-critical point in time when software must be *final*. There's no going back.

For buildings and structures, that's essential. In software, the metaphor made sense at one time too. When we shipped software on floppy disks and CDs, things had to be just right. There were huge cost and time implications for bugs. Projects were delayed for the sake of getting it perfect or for the sake of shoving in a new feature. I'll talk about what that does for morale in the next chapter.

Today, web-based applications aren't launched; they're uploaded, released, and pushed. Software lives and matures over time.

Once we've launched, iterations 2, 3, and 20 can come a few days or even a few hours later. Even the concept of formal version releases of software is antiquated. It made sense in the bygone days of shipping software on disk.

Today, we continuously integrate and constantly iterate. Unlike the auto industry, there's no need for mass recall. Today, a critical bug can be patched, tested, and deployed immediately. It's not version 2.0 anymore. It's version 2.0.12931. Or, it's simply *today's* version. Is anyone in the public eye really keeping track anymore?

Society is growing accustomed to iteration too. Did you see the new image gallery on Facebook? Did you see Google's new autosuggest feature? How about Twitter's new layout? Nobody warned us with a monthlong advertising campaign. New changes just *appear* now. IMVU,[1] a popular 3D-chat application, boasts more than 100 million registered users, and it ships releases 50 times *a day*.

---

1. http://www.imvu.com

In today's landscape, the initial launch shouldn't feel like the end-all and be-all like it once did or still does in many other industries. It's just one of hundreds (if not thousands) of mini-releases that take place during the life span of software. Keeping that perspective can relieve the mental pressure of launching software.

Unfortunately, this mentality can be easily abused. Don't use this change of construct as an excuse for being lazy or leaving loose ends untied. The launch of an application should be very, very good before others have at it. The big things need to be right. Proper security needs to be in place. But the small stuff, the stuff that is OK to fix afterward, shouldn't keep you from releasing software. You'll be surprised how often things you thought were important when you launched suddenly aren't...now that it's out there.

You still ought to celebrate when software launches. Take your team out to that fancy dinner. But don't spend all your emotional currency on just the wedding. There's an entire relationship you'll have with software afterward. There's time to make adjustments, add a family of new features, and right wrongs.

Launch is just another point in software's life. Not the end-all and be-all.

Essay 4

The "Ivory Tower" Architect Is a Myth

I've never liked the idea that technical architects should stop coding.

In physical architecture, architects perch in an ivory tower, living in a world of only planning. They don't hammer in the nails or solder joints together. Requiring architects to do the physical work of drilling holes and laying concrete is simply impractical. Architecting and developing are two distinct career tracks.

The Corporate Ladder Leads to Less Code

In our industry, we work our way up to the role of a technical architect by actually developing—by doing the "physical" work of building applications. But in most organizations, as we move up the software development ladder, we write less code. We immerse ourselves more with planning than with discovering the problems on the front line. We concern ourselves more about an overall vision and less about the intimate details of code. As an industry, we've held on to the notion that architects should plan and developers should develop.

This creates the false perception that once we've reached a certain level, programming is no longer where we're most valuable. Just leave the dirty work to the junior developers! At the same time, it pushes lower-level programmers away from thinking about the overall goals and direction of the project. They're asked to concentrate just on the implementation. The architect-developer model makes both parties less accountable for the application as a whole.

When we split up roles into the somewhat arbitrary hierarchy of those who think about the technical "big picture" and those who think only in if statements, for loops, and markup, we fracture two disciplines that belong intimately together.

Pure technical architects can take a guess at the best architecture, the best design pattern, or the best practice. It's only when they're knee-deep in code that they discover where the real challenges exist. At the same time, the developer who isn't given the reins to think at a high level also doesn't get the chance to voice a second opinion. Often, it's the guy who's doing the actual implementation who can see the bumps ahead most clearly.

We've taken the architect-developer analogy too far. The corporate ladder in the software industry needs a better analogy.

To build a building, architects architect and developers develop. Traditional architects know how to create elaborate plans and specs in fine detail. But they don't build. It's simply not reasonable. The separation between those who think at a high level and those who work in the trenches is largely for practical reasons.

In software, it doesn't have to be that way. Great developers can live both "in the trenches" and "at a high level" at the same time. Sure, an architect might spend most of her time thinking at a high level, but she should be involved in development a little to get the full picture.

Making Time for Code

In many technical organizations, what I've proposed thus far just isn't feasible. Most technical architects have a full-time job in meetings with other groups in the company. They're often brought in to client phone calls to discuss all kinds of technical challenges that face a software project. Where's the time to code, anyway?

A few months after I started one of my full-time web developer gigs, we hired a new senior architect. Adam came in and set a very different tone among our group of young web developers. Despite all the normal duties he took on in his role, it was clear his passion lived in code. Immediately, I felt like I was talking to just another programmer, albeit one a lot smarter and wiser than I. Our architect-developer relationship became my personal mentorship.

On our first project, an extranet for a major law firm, Adam mentioned something about code generation. To me, it sounded a bit sci-fi. However, as I would soon find out, the underlying server-side objects, queries, and methods I was going to write by hand were mainly algorithmic. We could largely deduce them from the extranet's database schema. Instead of plodding ahead with a brute-force approach to development, Adam suggested I focus on building out custom forms and screens while he began writing a code generator. He did this for a few weeks on his one-hour train ride to and from the office each day. In a few weeks' time, we had a rudimentary but powerful tool to generate a lot of the stuff I would've written manually.

Whatever time we lost with our little divergence into code generation, we quickly recouped as we began using the code generator. Each time we changed our database schema, he'd run his little magic app that would rewrite all the code I needed to keep building the application. It wasn't long before the effort Adam made in writing his tool more than paid back the cost in writing it. And this was a tool we could use again and again.

So, while I was still very much the lead developer on the project, Adam had a large stake in the development. If I needed some different bits of algorithmic code, he'd work on adding those features to the generator on train rides home. The next day, I'd have a fresh set of code that I wouldn't have to ever write by hand again. Much of what I learned in those first few months I keep with me today.

As you work your way up the programmer chain of command, from developer to architect, don't forget that code is the glue that binds each role. It may not be a train ride. Maybe it's an hour or two you can devote, at work, to only writing code. You'll see ways of committing yourself to code-only time in Essay 23, *Create "Off-Time" with Your Team*, on page 54. In the end, regardless of where you are in the development hierarchy, keep coding. It's where you're most valuable.

Essay 5

Throw Away Your Old Code

Recently, one of my colleagues, Mustafa, mentioned that I was "doing it again." I was *code hoarding*: commenting out code that I wasn't really planning on ever using again. I just didn't have the heart to delete it right then, even though we version control all of our source code (and you *absolutely* should be doing the same). Since I could always get that old code back anyway, there was no reason to be commenting out code when I could just delete it.

Code hoarding is one of many habits that seems right on the surface. It's a carryover from other staple engineering principles that aren't really relevant to programming. If we were building a car, we would probably save all our scrap metal because we could reuse it later. It would be stupid just to dump it. Labor and material are really critical in traditional engineering. In the physical world, it's much easier to work with something that's almost right than to rip it apart and start over.

In programming, we tend to put too much weight on those elements. Is our work really labor intensive? Not really. Typing isn't that strenuous. What about material? Last time I checked, we don't have a shortage of keystrokes.

At the same time, code hoarding ends up actually *creating* more obstacles. The reality is, most of the time, I never uncomment code that I commented out days or weeks ago. Instead, the blobs of monochromatic gibberish get dispersed around the actual code I'm writing at the moment. It's annoying to look at. Every time I work around the old code, it's distracting me from what matters right now.

Even if I do decide to re-implement something I wrote a while back, the code I commented out usually doesn't fit properly anyway. Maybe I've moved that piece of logic somewhere else. Objects or methods I reference in the old code may have changed. Trying to resuscitate old code means I spend more time jerry-rigging things than writing it correctly and cleanly again. The code I wrote last week was written by a version of me that only knew what last week's application looked like.

By deleting code instead of hoarding it in comments, we keep the codebase lean. What's on the page should reflect exactly how the application works right now. Nothing more, nothing less. By getting rid of old code *now*, there are no extraneous bits of gibberish to leap over when we're in the middle of programming. We don't have to wonder, later, whether that huge glob of commented-out but seemingly important code is really all that important still.

Diversification Over Specialization

In software, we can be the designer, the programmer, and the database administrator. We can be well versed in PHP, Java, .NET, C++, Python, and SQL while knowing our way around HTML, CSS, JavaScript, and Flash. But very few of us cross the line from user interface to backend comfortably.

In traditional architecture, it's not practical for the electrician to also be the cement pourer or for the bricklayer to also be the pipe fitter. They are specialties in and of themselves. They also occur in physically different places. The situation requires a group of specialized doers honing each craft separately for intellectual and practical reasons.

But transporting that same philosophy to our industry doesn't hold its weight. The tool sets we work within live on the screen right in front of us. If we're currently working in SQL, we don't have to go somewhere else to write HTML or to create an image in Photoshop. We simply switch programs on our computers. There is no physical barrier between any of our programming disciplines.

In addition, many software concepts transcend languages and, oftentimes, disciplines. Model-View-Controller (MVC) is an application architecture adopted in many UI platform applications, such as Adobe Flex's Cairngorm platform, along with many server-side development frameworks, such as .NET. Programming languages today have an extraordinary amount of overlap. Design patterns and refactoring are ideas that live everywhere in the programming landscape.

At my company, most of our development team knows multiple programming languages and splits time between the frontend and backend. It helps us even out everyone's workload because we're all adept at working on all layers of an application.

A .NET developer, an HTML standards whiz kid, and a data modeling expert can all live within the same person. We may have an expertise and interest in one or the other, but there's no reason we can't be great at many disciplines.

"I used to be in advanced business platform solutions; now I just make stuff work."

Why can't great programmers also be great user interface designers? All too often I hear a programmer instantly denounce even the possibility that she could also be a great visual designer. Conceptually, designing user interfaces is not that far off the map from designing a sound software architecture. Great, functional UIs are about clear affordances, organization, scalability, and intention. They have many of the same qualities we cherish in software design.

The reverse is also true. Too few talented user interface designers consider themselves capable of becoming great programmers. Perhaps programmers look at user interface design as making things "pretty" and designers look at programming as writing a lot of "technical stuff." Meanwhile, they have so much more in common than that.

In the end, the goals of software design from both the interface level and the engine are the same. There is no reason why we can't be great at multiple disciplines.

Metaphors Hide Better Ways of Working

We've seen why metaphors can hurt how we approach software. When we take them too far, we develop habits built around false pretenses. Metaphors are a double whammy. Not only do they make us do things less efficiently, but they keep us from thinking about *better ways* of doing things.

Wireframes and detailed specifications take time away from building and reviewing the real thing. They don't take advantage of the opportunities we have to constantly iterate. They make us think through the entire process of writing code without actually having written any code yet.

The over-emphasis on launch hides the fact that software today can be modified and redistributed with relative ease. We don't "ship" software anymore. We download it off the Internet, or the software itself is entirely web-based. When launch dates get pushed back because features absolutely need to be crammed in, developer morale suffers. It's a complete buzz kill for a development team.

The traditional roles in software development, between architects, developers, and project managers, inhibit those who have talents in multiple areas. You can be a great visionary, a thoughtful programmer, and a clear communicator at the same time. Following the metaphor too closely inhibits really talented people from all the opportunities this industry provides.

One way to circumvent this problem is to find a more appropriate analogy. Software development might be closer to writing a novel or composing music. Consider how these kinds of professionals "plan" their work.

An author might write a chapter outline to get a general guide about what she wants to write about. But after that, she starts writing the real thing. Then she edits and repeats

—a word change here or an entire chapter removed there. Writing is a lot more like how we program.

A musician doesn't write sheet music for months and then hope the notes sound right. He plays and plays and finds a riff that works. He might have a few lines of lyrics and then find the right chords around it, or vice versa. He builds the song in pieces and tests it in pieces.

In both cases, the cost of materials is cheap. Paper and pen are readily available. Guitars don't get paid by the note because sound is cheap. Just the same, code is our own cheap material. Once we have our development environment set up, there is no material cost of writing code.

So, use our traditional metaphors for development as a stake in the ground, when you're not quite sure how to approach a software problem or when there's not enough information to make sound decisions. But once you've run with the metaphors for a while, look up. See where they're still helping *and* where they might be hurting your process.

With this knowledge in place, we're now keenly aware of whether the processes we abide by actually work. The next step is about the long-term. How can we keep ourselves motivated throughout the course of our development career? Next, let's discuss a few ways we can sustain our motivation.

CHAPTER 3

Motivation

Regardless of how skilled you are, if you're not motivated to write code, get out. Accountants might get through writing up a spreadsheet just fine without motivation; a cashier can get by his day without passion. But unmotivated developers kill a software project.

Motivation must be sustainable. It must be unearthed and cultivated continuously throughout development. What keeps you coding with passion at the beginning of a project might not be your source of inspiration at the finish line. Different things can get you going at different points in the process of building software.

Sustaining motivation isn't unique to software. We see it all the time in the media. The star athlete who signed the big, multimillion-dollar contract now doesn't give his full effort during a game. The band we grew up loving now starts cashing in by churning out mediocre albums. Many celebrities burn out even with the guarantee of ridiculous wealth. It's proof that one thing alone isn't enough to sustain motivation.

We need different ways to keep passion running through our veins. A food critic's review keeps a chef on her toes. But so does a busy restaurant and a happy staff. The right tools also help sustain motivation. Show a great chef a quality set of knives and some fresh ingredients, and you'll see amazing things happen. The motivation to run a restaurant comes from all different kinds of sources. So does building software.

The Perks Are in the Work

In this industry, long-lasting motivation doesn't come from the perks. Indeed, a big salary and a free lunch are nice. So is a foosball table. In the end, long-lasting motivation comes from the *work we do*. Every passionate programmer I've ever met is far more excited to tell me about an elegant solution to some technical problem they've spent hours agonizing over than that 10 percent raise they just received at their corporate coding gig.

Perks Aren't Motivators in the Long Run

That's why I'm baffled when, time after time, I watch people settle for that new yet completely uninspiring gig with the slightly larger salary and the promise of a bigger bonus, especially when it's the young and carefree among us with only the monthly rent to pay.

"I dunno, lately I'm just not incentivized..."

Don't stick around at the corporate gig you hate just because they're luring you with more cash. Leave that kind of job mentality to people who are just coding for the money and waiting for the hours to pass until the next weekend.

If the difference between salary X and salary X * 1.05 is really the difference between a few more wild nights out on the town a year, go for the gig with the more interesting problems. Pick the job with the more impassioned employees. Go where you have a chance to *build something beautifully*, where the actual projects are at the center of everyone's interests. What you might trade in salary (if you need to at all) you'll more than earn back in happiness.

A telltale sign of a good company is how they approach their projects. Great projects have distinct, concrete goals. Great projects have either all the pieces in place or a plan to get them in place. Great projects are as ambitious as they are well thought out. Great projects have a defined time to deliver, rather than an undetermined amount of time and budget. These kinds of projects give work a purpose. Among the hundreds of programming projects I've worked on, all the great ones had these motivating qualities.

Perks Can Be Destructive

There's even evidence that superficial perks actually make our work less motivating. Yes, the carrots dangling in front of us might actually make us *less* passionate to do our work.

There is a wonderful TED talk given by *New York Times* best-selling author Dan Pink on the surprising science of motivation.[1] He argues that traditional motivational factors in business, like a big bonus, can succeed, but they succeed only on trivial tasks, like, say, entering data from one spreadsheet into another.[2]

In contrast, tasks that involve critical analysis and creative problem-solving, like the ones that we face every day, aren't aided by dangling a monetary prize over someone's head. In experiments that involved higher-level thinking, there was an *inverse* correlation between monetary incentive and performance: the greater the monetary reward given to a particular group of subjects, the *worse* they ended up doing.

---

1. http://www.ted.com/talks/dan_pink_on_motivation.html
2. If you want the long version, read his *Drive: The Surprising Truth About What Motivates Us* [Pin09].

Giving people extra rewards to accomplish a task that was already appealing at its core made the work less appealing!

For me, it doesn't matter all that much what I'm building. It could be a one-page website, a search engine, an online Rolodex, an interactive map, or a game. It could be used by millions or thousands or eight people. It could be a six-month build or a two-hour exercise. I could be mostly writing markup, working on UI, writing server-side code, or building a database. In the end, I'm passionate about my work when I know that I have a chance to *build something beautifully*.

When choosing that next gig, remember what really keeps us motivated for the long haul. It isn't the external perks; it's the work itself.

Essay 9

Begin Where You Love to Begin

Sometimes the hardest place to find motivation is at the very start. Thinking about code is easy. Software always compiles perfectly in our heads. We don't obsess over the hundreds of minor obstacles we'll face along the way. But once we commit to actually writing code, the entire game changes. Motivation can fade quickly.

The experience of writing software is not too different from writing this book. I spent far more time thinking about what I wanted to write about than actually writing. Writing can sometimes be a soul-sucking game of uninspired lines, mental blocks, and fatigue. It's hard to keep the juices flowing when I run into a gauntlet of personal demotivators.

Natalie Goldberg's *Writing Down the Bones* [Gol05] is an entire book on motivation for writers. She offers a simple tip for getting started. Instead of focusing on the big opening, start writing somewhere in the middle of the story. Begin at the point that's most interesting, right now. Don't try to write from the very beginning.

We spend so much time concerning ourselves with the big, attention-grabbing opener when, in reality, it's a rather insignificant portion of the entire story. There's a considerable amount of work after the opening paragraph. That's the approach I took for this book. Nothing was written linearly. In the beginning, I focused on a specific topic when that topic inspired me.

We can apply the same concept to building software. We don't have to start with the home page before the subpages or with the database before the business logic. Instead of starting software at the beginning, we can start at the place where we are most engaged. We have that luxury while many other builders don't. Unlike building houses, cars, or anything physical, we do not need to start anywhere specific. We can always *refactor* later. We may take a few circuitous routes, but if they are inspired rather than labored, we'll get more good work done faster.

So, if you have the freedom to be greedy about where to start writing software, be greedy. Pick a feature you find most interesting and work your way out from there.

This is especially helpful when you're about to embark on building a big piece of software. Rather than spend three days formulating a timeline and release schedule, commit those days to working on the part of the application that most interests you. A week in, you'll know how much motivation you really have, and you'll have a far better idea of when the other parts can fall into place.

If you find yourself quickly losing steam, you can cut your losses then. Still, more often than not, you'll find the daunting task of building software not so insurmountable. Three solid days (or a week) of building an application, and you'll know a lot more about what you're building and how quickly the rest can get done. Putting together a realistic timeline is much easier after you have a bit of inspired work under your belt.

Essay 10

Be Imperfect

Every passionate programmer cares, first and foremost, about her code. Code is our canvas. Although no user will ever look at our code, the passionate programmer labors over every line. Even when we know, full well, we're building a small app for a small audience, a lot of us still care that our applications will perform under the biggest of stages. We care about how our code might perform under the most severe of conditions. We make attempts to reduce excess calls to the server, to the service, and to the database.

And yet, to survive in this industry, we better not be perfectionists. There is no such thing as a perfect piece of software, especially web-based software. Our products live through our users. They morph as our user base grows. Features beget new features. Bugs beget new bugs. Trying to be perfect can become exhausting.

The approach a developer took the first day she wrote her first line of code is likely completely different from the approach she's taking today. Software changes over time. We build, tweak, iterate, and occasionally have to rewrite. So, we'd better be OK with that.

In development, there are often trade-offs between performance and coding simplicity or between perfect architecture and maintainability. There is no silver bullet to determine which way is necessarily the right way.

A great software developer is obsessive-compulsive yet accepts imperfection all the time. Trying to write "perfect code" is crippling. The quicker we can accept imperfection, the more motivated we'll be to keep moving forward with our work, and the more work we'll actually get done.

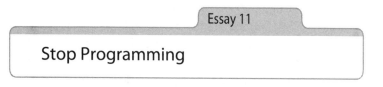

Stop Programming

You probably program too much.

Just when you've really gotten into your work, when your brain is entirely wrapped around your code, when your hands, eyes, and thoughts are working in harmony, stop. Look up. Think about when you're going to finish for the day. Look forward to shutting off your computer. Get outside a little.

Programming, for all its mental exercise, is a very comfortable physical activity. We usually program while sitting, and as the hours waste away, we slouch lower in our chairs. Some of us even eat and drink at our desks while we code away. We can tell just by examining our keyboards—the somewhat slick ones with a pound of crumbs under the keys.

This comfort is dangerous. It means we can do this for hours and hours and hours without realizing just how much we've exhausted our own resources.

When you hit that point where your code starts to get a bit sloppy—or, better yet, just before it—stop. Great programming is about maximizing the time you're working at your best, not the cumulative hours you spend in front of a screen.

Two hours of quality programming time is better than eight hours of struggle. We're far more susceptible to taking shortcuts or breaking standard conventions when we're coding tired. Those extra hours are spent creating bad code—code that we might regret the next day. So, cut all that programming time down, get outside, and live a little.

Essay 12

Test Your Work First Thing in the Morning

Test your software first thing in the morning. That's when you're the freshest and the most motivated to continue building something good.

During the day, we spend so much effort building software that we lose steam testing each piece we write. It gets hard to see the big picture as the day wears on. By late afternoon, we're too close to the software. Our perception of what makes sense or feels right now competes with fatigue. Also, fatigue makes us miss the small details.

Should this feature be here or there? Should we move this function to another screen? Will this make sense? Is this latest tweak really that important? At 5 p.m. (or, for the truly overworked, 2 a.m.), it's hard to know what our software feels like because we've been at it for too long.

However, at 9 a.m., fresh from a night's sleep, we can usually answer these questions better. Our mental cobwebs are gone. Before diving into the build, this is the best time to give our software the once-over.

In the morning, our software feels new again. We approach it less fettered by what's behind the scenes. We can consume it from a less biased viewpoint because we've had that time away.

The morning has a way of making us forget some of the copious details of code we may have obsessed about the night before. No longer preoccupied with the slightly inelegant implementation that made something work, our minds are totally devoted to what we see in front of us rather than thinking about what's happening underneath.

"I found these in your desk..."

When you test, start from the beginning. Don't dig into a particular section. Just experience it again. The night before, you may have been working on a piece of functionality that a real user may use only once or twice...or never. In the morning, focus on the things most people will use most of the time. It's a much better way to focus on the priorities of your software and focus on what needs fixing first.

Testing your software in the morning, before adding more code, is a great way to make sure you're still making good software. It's when you're the freshest.

Essay 13

Work Outside the Bedroom

I began building websites in my college dorm room in the late 1990s. By my senior year, my time was split two ways; I was taking a few courses to finish up my credits during the day, and I was freelancing in web design from my dorm room in the evenings. Homework? What homework?

While some of my contemporaries were working minimum wage at the dining hall or computer lab (remember those?), here I was, in my boxers, moving a mouse around the screen making five times as much per hour. My commute to bed was a step, or sometimes two steps on a bad day.

For awhile, I was living The Life. I was getting my degree and earning a respectable salary for a college student working from his bedroom.

The fall after I graduated, I began work at a small technology firm in Chicago. I started just as the dot-com bubble burst and the American economy went into a tailspin. Six weeks into the job, my position there also burst. I went back to live with my parents. Suddenly I was a 22-year-old adult picking up a few freelance web projects, again, from the comfort of my bedroom.

The first few weeks felt great. After the initial honeymoon, being in my pajamas felt kind of different. I wasn't in school anymore. My friends weren't down the hall or just up campus. It was just me and my desktop. Without other required diversions in place (like going to class and finishing my degree), work filled up all of my time.

It wasn't that I was sweating away eight hours a day; it was that I was working in short spurts throughout the day. A couple hours of real work in the morning, a snack break, a few hours of daytime court television, a few more hours of work, a run, a meal, and—oh, yes—a few more hours of work to cap off the evening. My five to five hours of billable time was spread thinly across twelve to fourteen hours. There was no separation between work life and real life. I wasn't working passionately or efficiently anymore.

As Parkinson's law states, "Work expands so as to fill the time available for its completion." When I was able to be "at work" any hour of the day, there was a whole lot of time to fill up. Suddenly, my 40-hour work week turned into a 168-hour mush of work, sleep, and kinda-being-around-work.

Working from home is a luxury. Most people would trade a two-hour commute for a fall-out-of-bed commute. But if you have that luxury, don't code in your bedroom. Or your living room, for that matter. Find a confined area to work, preferably a second room, where you can physically leave from after your workday is over. Shut the door at the end of the day, hang up the "Closed" sign, and get on with the rest of your life until tomorrow.

That's how you really live The Life.

First Impressions Are Just That

As software goes, how important is a user's first impression? Especially an unfavorable one? I don't think they are very important at all. We shouldn't let them instantly curtail our motivation.

No doubt, bad first impressions may be a sign that something really is wrong with our software. But there are two things I've learned that account for many bad first impressions.

Bad First Impressions Can Come from Unfamiliarity

Sometimes bad first impressions come from simply not having used the software before. We should really take these types of impressions with a grain of salt. For instance, the first time I used Gmail, I thought to myself:

> These emails, they're like mini-forums. They're like threads of discussion...not email. Interesting. Strange. Do I like it? No. Yes. I don't know...maybe?

Gmail email threads were initially a strange concept. I heard many people rave about it, but I heard an equal number rip it to shreds. Fast-forward a few months later. I stopped hearing about it altogether. Here's a more typical conversation you might have with someone who uses Gmail today:

Male in red cap: *Hey dude, do you use Gmail?*

Male in blue cap: *Yeah.*

Male in red cap: *What do you think?*

Male in blue cap: *It's fine. Lately it's been slow. Anyway, let's go grab some beers!*

It turns out that both types of email systems work for me, for these two fine gentlemen above, and for the vast majority of the world. After a while, we stopped obsessing over it. In fact, today, I use both Outlook and Gmail. I also know lots of others who use both a non-Gmail email client and Gmail. When I use Outlook, I expect normal, old-school email. When I use Gmail, I expect "special forum-like mail madness." In the end, I'm comfortable with both.

"I'm more of a late adopter."

I'll admit it. It takes some guts to try to redefine paradigms as firmly implanted in society as email. In our line of work, fortunately, the stakes are a lot smaller. Radio buttons or drop-down list? Search box on every page or just some pages? The likely answer? Yes. Yes. Yes. And yes. In the end, when we are accustomed to seeing the same software over and over, there's a good chance we'll get comfortable with whatever design decisions we first had a problem with.

I hear the naysayers knocking loudly. Am I really saying that users should conform to software, instead of the other way around? Am I really suggesting that our initial reactions to software are not important? Is this coming from the same guy who helped bring you *Flash Application Design Solutions: The Flash Usability Handbook* [CB06]? Yes it is!

I'm not saying that first impressions carry no weight. But those initial impulse reactions we have to something we see for the very first time are often just reactions to the unfamiliar. We're naturally daunted by something new. Yet, too often, as developers, we take those initial user reactions too seriously.

Bad First Impressions Aren't Always Based on What's Important

Here's the other problem: sometimes bad first impressions are not indicative of what's really important.

If Google just opened shop and I was a usability tester, here's what my first impressions might be:

- The "Google Search" button should flip with "I'm Feeling Lucky" because I'm used to clicking the rightmost button when I submit information, and I'm usually going to search for something real rather than press my luck.

- I don't get what "I'm Feeling Lucky" is actually going to do. That's confusing. There should be instruction there as to what might happen when I click it.

- I had to go hunting for a while to find the advanced search option. Oh, and that advanced search page was hard to use.

- The navigation links at the bottom should be above the search bar, because that's where I'm used to seeing navigation.

Ask me now, and I can refute most of my initial concerns. I've gotten used to the placement of the search button. After using the "I'm Feeling Lucky" button a couple times, I now know it just takes the first search off the list and sends you right there. The advanced search feature? I *never* use it anyway, so who cares if it's not that easy to use? And ditto on those links at the bottom. I'm glad they're underneath the search box instead of at the top.

First impressions are often skewed because we don't really get how we'll ultimately conform to the software. Initially, something we think might be important, like an advanced search option, ends up not being important at all. With something that's a little off from what we're accustomed to, like the order of the "Search" and "I'm Feeling Lucky" buttons, we simply get acclimated to after a short period of time.

So, when you're confronted with negative feedback from your customers, clients, or co-workers, stick to your guns. Explain why you did the things you did. Ask them to let your work simmer for a few days. Don't let that initial rush of feedback demotivate you.

If those problems still persist, then perhaps there really is a flaw in your application. But you'll be surprised how many of those initial negative impressions often just fade away.

Essay 15

The Emotional Value of Launch

In the previous chapter, I talked about launch. In today's development, launch is just one of many releases in the life span of software. But launch is significant for another reason: a launch date gives a powerful dose of motivation.

Why? Because we know our software is no longer waiting on the sidelines; it is alive and ready and is a huge lift to the ego.

The good feeling that comes from *finishing* the first phase has a huge implication on how well and efficiently we'll *continue* to do our work in the future. Contrast that with the soul-sinking feeling we get from the endless tweaking of software still not deemed ready for prime-time.

Sometimes, though, we're scared to launch. Launch means that our precious application is now at the mercy of the masses. What will they say? As we saw in the previous essay, whatever they say at first might not be what they think down the road. Even if there are critical changes that have to be made, *we can make them*. Very few add-ons, removals, or logic shifts are undoable. Good programmers prepare themselves for this all the time. The basis of design patterns, methods on refactoring, and best practices is largely to accommodate for change in the future.

So, get your software to launch as soon as you reasonably can. You'll find out more about how to ensure your launch date doesn't keep slipping away in our next chapter on productivity.

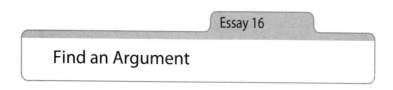

Essay 16

Find an Argument

There are other ways to stay motivated than simply coding away on the next great application.

Find an argument. Find a topic that you passionately agree with. Better yet, find one you unabashedly disagree with. Then go speak about it. Explain why your way works in intricate detail.

Get involved in a local Meetup.com group or apply to speak at a conference. Don't think you're not good enough or ready to be heard; if you can find a topic you're passionate about, you're ready. You don't have to be a rock-star programming hero, the one with the 50,000 Twitter followers and the über-successful business. For right now, you can just be yourself. What's wonderful about the web community is that your voice is built, first, on substance. If you have something to say, you *can* be heard.

If the very thought of speaking is making your palms sweat, then *write*. Writing gives you the chance to fumble your words 1,000 times before you finally get it just perfect. You can start with a blog or contact other more established bloggers to write guest posts. You'll be surprised how receptive the community at-large is.

In need of an argument? Here are few polarizing topics that might get you started:

- Is it ever OK to use <TABLE />s in your HTML markup for anything other than tabular content? Many markup purists say no. Maybe you can say yes and explain why.

- Is Adobe Flash still relevant in the rich web application space, or has enough advancement been made with HTML5, CSS3, and JavaScript to make Flash irrelevant?

- Are object-relational mappers (ORMs) better to use than raw SQL? Many would argue that ORMs are almost always inefficient when you make more complex database queries. Others argue that the simplicity ORMs provide to the developer is worth the trade-off.

- Is Model-View-Controller architecture the best way to architect all applications? Some would say that it's a bloated architecture and simply using a standard page model works better.

- How important is usability testing and A/B testing for web applications? Some argue it's overhyped and the effort of running studies of your application isn't worth the up-front cost and time.

As we've seen throughout this chapter, motivation can come in many forms. It doesn't have to live just within the boundaries of code but can also be how we approach our jobs when we're away from the desk. Even a good argument can keep our passion running high.

If you can stay motivated throughout the course of your development career, you'll get productive too. Let's find out how we can turn our motivation into sustained productivity.

CHAPTER 4

Productivity

Motivation may be what we need to get started, but productivity is the tangible measure of success. This chapter is about maintaining a consistent level of impassioned work every day.

The corporate world, as it does with just about any concept, equates productivity to some calculable metric. In this case, it's a metric like *utilization* or *throughput*. Productivity is often distilled into a formula that determines how *much* work we do or how *many* things we juggle at once, not the quality of our work. Real productivity is about quality work.

Take multitasking, for instance. It's the quintessential act of feeling like we're being productive but rarely a great way to actually do good work. "Working through lunch" is one of these acts. How much quality code is really being written typing with one pointer finger while the other hand grips that footlong sandwich?

More importantly, that's just not an enjoyable way to work. Leave your desk. Eat your lunch in peace, and get some fresh air. The code will be there when you come back.

Essay 17

Just Say "No" to the Pet Project

Every one of us has a pet project archive. It could be software we started and saw partway through but never quite finished. It could be code that began strong but came to a screeching halt because more pressing issues came up. Other work got in the way, or we simply lost interest.

Pet projects fail when there are no time constraints and nothing is on the line if we don't succeed. When a launch date is "one of these days," we likely won't be finishing it anytime soon. Some of us seem to spend years mulling over that next great idea instead of first deciding on a specific amount of time to build it.

How about just three months? Jack Dorsey spent less than that from initial concept to launch of the first version of a little-known SMS messaging service that later would be called Twitter.[1] Imagine if, instead, he had spent years and years on development instead of the short burst from start to launch. Things might have turned out differently.

Timing Is Everything

That's why *time* is the most important parameter in maintaining a passion for writing software. With a pet project, it's fine to start writing code for amusement and learning. However, when we're ready to turn it into something real, we need to define our time boundaries. Answering the following turns a project into something real:

- How much time will I spend working on this project each day, and how many days will I spend each week?
- When can I show a mostly ready product to someone else?
- What day will I launch this to the public?
- What day will I release my first major iteration?

---

1.   http://en.wikipedia.org/wiki/Twitter

The first question creates sustainable, daily expectations. Maybe it's just two hours a day and three days a week. It just has to be consistent. From 3 p.m. to 5 p.m. each afternoon is better than "whenever I find a gap in my schedule." Spread it evenly too. Mondays, Wednesdays, and Fridays might be a better set of days to work than lumping all three days over the weekend. That leaves too large a gap between sessions, and you'll waste a lot of that extra time refreshing your memory about where you previously left off. Finally, make your schedule achievable. Making a habit of saying "I'll put it off today and make it up tomorrow" gets stale really fast.

The second question gives us a deadline for test-ready software. It's a stake in the ground: a short time from now where our co-worker, friend, or spouse gets a crack at what we've done. It helps us to work backward to figure out how much time we need to do our work between now and then. Couple this with how much time we spend per day and week, and we'll know how much time we need to do every coding session.

The third question gets us ready for "good enough" software, which is software that has all the big things right and is ready for the general public. It's launch-ready. The time between the previous date and this one is where we fix the bugs that are critical to get right, not the hundreds of minuscule feature additions we all want but can live without for a few weeks.

And that's where the answer to the fourth question comes in. It sets us up for everything after launch. We've launched, and now we need to set up a time to push new releases. Perhaps it's a week after launch or less. Because it's web-based software, it can be just a few days (or even hours) after launch. Once we actually have gotten to this stage, we're off and running.

These time constraints create the walls we need to fill in with work. It helps us define our most important features. It gives purpose to each moment we put into our software. Without rigid time constraints, we can go on noodling forever wondering whether we've made something just right. Instead of getting ready to deliver something, we'll be tweaking each step for as long as we please. Productivity dries up when we don't have that sense of urgency. Time constraints keep us progressing.

Set a Deadline, Even If It's Arbitrary

Our company's first product, DoneDone,[2] began as one of my pet projects. DoneDone is a simple web-based, bug-tracking tool that focuses on clarity and a simple workflow over complex features. I started writing it because we didn't like the other bug tracker we were using that was costing us $120 every month. It was gaudy in places we wanted less. It was missing some small things that would've made our process more efficient. I knew I could do something better. If we were willing to pay for our current bug tracker, others would certainly pay for this.

For the first few weeks, I worked with only ideas. No wire-frames or specs. I just wrote code, built interfaces, tested, refined, and wrote some more. I was still in the honeymoon period of development. Though I was directionless, the thought of making money off a product was enough motivation to start.

Fast-forward a few months later. It was November. Client work began to pick up again, and naturally, my pet project got shuffled to the back of the priority line. Every few days, I might carve out a couple of hours to build DoneDone, but those hours were sluggish and unproductive. Most of my time was spent reacquainting myself with what I had done before. Because those time periods weren't consistent, it was hard to decide what I should work on when I suddenly found myself free.

Instead, I needed a new approach. As a business, we had to treat DoneDone with the urgency of a client project. What was the difference between this project and projects we'd done for other clients? It was simply that we were our *own* client. And just like a client project, we needed dates: a date to release DoneDone internally, a date to launch the product to the public, and dates to release iterations thereafter.

2.　http://www.getdonedone.com

In the end, I decided we would launch DoneDone on April 15, 2009. Perhaps there was some poetic connection with the fact that it was the same day the IRS collects our taxes. Frankly, it was just an arbitrary date, about six months away, that felt like the right amount of time—not too much, not too little. There was a lot of work to be done, but if I used 50 percent of my workday on DoneDone and brought in a couple people to pitch in every now and then, we could get this project off the ground. A pet project suddenly became a real project.

With a deadline set, we could fill in that time with a requisite amount of work. We needed to add the payment gateway, figure out our cost structure, build a marketing site, and clean up our feature set. Everything had a time and a place. That sense of urgency—and productivity—came back.

After we launched, there were certainly other features to add. Looking back on it, it's hard to imagine DoneDone ever not having them. We did not have an email-to-ticket system or a tagging system for issues, both core pieces of the product today, but they simply weren't mission-critical for launch. We focused on the most important features that a bug-tracking tool that took six months to build would require. Over the next ninety days, we released ten new updates of DoneDone.

Have I really written a whole essay about setting deadlines? Yes. In all its unrevolutionariness, it's amazing how having a hard date in your head is the difference between work that gets done and work that escapes into La La Land. Deadlines keep your work relevant. When you let your project bleed from months into even years, your product might not have the intended worth it had when you began.

Deadlines create a sense of urgency that gets you to the finish line. They give you the push you need even if you have no one else breathing down your neck.

Essay 18

Constrain All of Your Parameters

In the previous essay, we saw how time constraints turn pet projects into real products. But time isn't the only parameter we can constrain. All software costs money to build. So, put a cap on it. Capping cost makes us creative. It helps us figure out a more efficient way of using our resources.

Consider all the sad stories of lottery winners who go from working nine-to-five jobs to suddenly having more cash than they know what to do with. Rather than save their money, they go off throwing it away on things like...yachts. They give away thousands to long-lost relatives. After a while, many of them go into debt and are worse off than had they not won at all. They didn't realize a million dollars is still a *finite* amount of money. Even though the monetary walls are spread further apart, they are still there.

This, too, is why so many venture capitalist–backed start-ups have failed. Back in the original dot-com era, a VC throwing fifty million dollars to a group of guys with a lofty idea but no proof of success was commonplace. With so much money in play, it was easy to decide that the necessary next step was a big downtown office, a few hundred out-of-college new hires, and a board of directors. After all, if a VC was going to give you that much money, you better do *something* with it.

When the market set the value of untested companies so high, it inflated the worth of the idea rather than the worth of the work. It wasn't necessary to get a small product out in the market early to see whether it had any promise. Tweaking a few features and redeploying software didn't merit another million dollars. Instead of using the size of their customer base to determine the size of their web servers, some companies would just buy up the entire server farm and wait for the customer base to grow.

"I like it! I like it a *lot!*"

A bottomless bank vault took the urgency out of succeeding. Many companies found ways of being productive, but that kind of productivity wasn't focused on the product.

Had Kozmo.com, a VC-backed company that delivered food and entertainment goods to your doorstep *for no delivery fee* been given only a few hundred thousand dollars to operate, it may have felt the urgency to turn a profit a bit quicker. Instead, Kozmo.com blew through several hundred million dollars, expanding its highly unprofitable service to nine major U.S. cities.[3] By the end of the third year, Kozmo.com liquidated. By not having to worry about a profitable product early on, Kozmo never got a chance to adjust a promising idea into a solid product.

When we don't have the walls around us, whether they are walls around time, cost, or a feature set, we lose sight of reality. We make questionable decisions because nothing is forcing us to choose wisely. Our productivity isn't spent on the important things.

If you want to develop great software, set up and obey the walls around you. Make every step you take a step toward building a more successful application. There are not enough resources to do anything else.

---

3. http://money.cnn.com/galleries/2010/technology/1003/gallery.dot_com_busts/9.html

Essay 19

Cut the Detail Out of the Timeline

In twelve years of software development, I've never seen a project go exactly as planned.

Functionality changes. Unanticipated obstacles arise. Sometimes things that we think might take a week actually take three. Yet, all too often, we put too much *detail* into a project timeline. Putting a delivery deadline on every little component means we become slaves to our own timeline. We've decided how long every single step will take without having taken any of the steps yet. It's impossible to come up with the perfect plan at the very beginning.

So, when you begin your plan, plan with less detail.

Build timeline deliverables in sizeable chunks, not in small breadcrumbs. If you're estimating an eight-week project, give yourself eight weekly deliverables rather than forty daily ones. Instead of defining when each individual inter-action of your application can be delivered, decide when a complete section can be delivered. In the end, it's the same amount of time but with fewer checkpoints in between.

When our timelines get too detailed and our delivery dates become too frequent, there's no wiggle room to experiment or reconsider the details of an application as we go. We're forced to stick to a rigid schedule of guessed tasks, as if an ignorant micro-manager were hovering over us constantly. Then when the timing of a few of those small tasks goes awry, suddenly the entire timeline feels like it's crumbling right in front of us. That's not motivating, nor is it how good software gets built.

A lot of front-end developers approach screen design in drastically different ways. Some like to mock up a screen perfectly in Photoshop and then translate the visual into HTML and CSS. Others like to start directly in code. Some like to focus strictly on the markup structure first before putting in a single color or font size. Others need to see the design unfold as they build the structure. Some start by building for the lowest common denominator and work their way up. Others start with the optimal screen resolution and work on gracefully degrading their layouts later.

Setting a deadline for delivering completed screens is a good milestone. But making deadlines for all the in-between components specifically (just the HTML or just the CSS) isn't. It doesn't give a developer the liberty to work the way she works most efficiently.

Giving ourselves a reasonable amount of time between deliverables enables us to play. It breaks down a large project into bite-size mini-projects where we *still* get the chance to approach the build the way we want. It gives us the chance to iterate a few times before our next deadline. A week (or two) before our next deliverable gives us the opportunity to make a few mistakes and still recover.

Essay 20

Improve Your Product in Two Ways Daily

Let's not sugarcoat programming. At times, development can get dull. There are moments when I'd like to do anything else, like perform open-heart surgery on an endangered animal.

In the proverbial dog days of development, sustainable productivity has to come from really small victories. The simple satisfaction of coding or those delusions of fame won't keep us productive all the time. There has to be a daily nugget of inspiration—a baseline motivator that exists even when the more general motivators grow stale.

For the first year of our company, I spent a large amount of time building a web-based data modeling application called X2O. To this day, X2O creates the application framework for every web project we build at We Are Mammoth. It generates an interface to build an application's data model and maintains the database, data access layer, and web services so we can rapidly build customized database-driven apps.

X2O is an application with lofty goals. It is wildly complex in places, with a whole lot going on underneath the hood. Broken down, it's a synthesis of several dozen applications that help generate different parts of a custom application. Maintaining passion to keep building it is hard because each of these apps is a big application in itself. Building big stuff like this requires small victories.

While I was knee-deep in development, I put a new rule into my day-to-day efforts on X2O: make two things better about the software each day.

They didn't have to be big improvements. They could be very little ones, such as creating more elegant, friendly error messages on the UI or getting rid of stale code. Even making sure all the methods have good comments was an improvement. Some days I'd have the energy to tackle a big task and a little one. Other days, I'd do maybe two minor ones. In the end, every day I knew that X2O *that day* was quantifiably better than X2O *the day before*.

There's significance in the number two as well. One improvement can sometimes be daunting. Which one do we choose? One is also too close to zero. One makes it easy to convince ourselves that we could skip today and make up that extra one tomorrow. On the other hand, three is a lot to sustain every day. Two is a magical number.

Deciding to make your product better in two ways every day is a good mental exercise to keep those large projects moving forward. In a working week, you'll have ten better things to say about your product than you do now. In a working month, you'll have forty better things to say about your product than you do now.

Essay 21

Invest in a Good Work Environment

Ever notice the difference between a cheap roll of Saran Wrap and an expensive roll? For spendthrifts, it's hard to justify paying twice as much money for a roll of sticky plastic. But the differences are obvious. A great roll is easy to tug. It doesn't cling too vigorously on itself but sticks snuggly over a bowl. Most importantly, a great roll tears off easily.

At the grocery store, it's tempting to opt for the cheap brand; after all, we're talking about *Saran Wrap*. But the few dollars we save initially is paid back each time we have a frustrating experience ripping off that stretched, unsticky piece of plastic.

Multiply the Saran Wrap experience with everything else we might do in the kitchen. When every tool is less than optimal, our overall experience is marred by little moments of nonproductivity. The more little things that get in our way each time we try to get work done, the less productive we'll be.

This same philosophy is especially true for us programmers. Productivity depends on every *little* thing that surrounds where we work. Our work environment should do everything to minimize that distraction.

A Really Fast, Versatile Machine Is Worth the Extra Cost

That's why it's critical to invest in good hardware. The financial costs we put in up front will invariably pay off every day, in the currency of *productivity*.

I recently upgraded from using a seven-year-old Dell Inspiron 9300 laptop running Windows XP to a MacBook Pro running Windows 7 on Parallels. The investment was monetarily substantial, but for that singular, one-time down payment, I now reap the benefits every minute I'm working.

There was nothing wrong with my old laptop. I could upgrade its memory for a hundred bucks and keep tolerating it for another few years. However, in many small ways, it was becoming similar to that average roll of Saran Wrap. There were small disadvantages that I was paying for every coding session.

With my new laptop, I can now take advantage of both platforms at once. I can run a much speedier version of Photoshop on the Mac, in a pinch, while still working on a .NET application with Visual Studio on the Windows side. Plus, I can browser test on both PC and Mac without having to set up multiple browsers on one of those cast-off computers—the ones companies typically denote the "Browser Testing Machine."

"Still nothing. You sure this is the
best computer we have?"

The advantages aren't limited just to the software. I've even fallen in love with the keyboard. The keys are flat and thin. They have just the right responsiveness to the touch. They let me type more fluidly and seamlessly as compared to a traditional bulkier keyboard. I make far fewer typos on my new keyboard.

Now, consider the impact of each typo I *don't* make. That's one less moment of having to break my train of thought. That's one less moment of having to move my eyes from the screen to the keyboard to retrace my steps. That's one less moment of, then, having to remind myself where I left off in my train of thought.

Suppose I make only four fewer typos a day with my new keyboard (in reality, I'm sure it's much more than that). In a given year, that's about 1,000 fewer minor interruptions while I code, all for the cost of just one new keyboard.

Invest in More Real Estate

In the kitchen, more countertop space is never a bad thing. When we're making a recipe that involves a few dozen ingredients and a couple bulky appliances, a vast expanse of area in front of us is essential. That way, we don't have to stack items on top of each other. We can organize our tools in different areas of space as we please.

More countertop space means less chance we accidentally set raw ingredients on top of cooked ingredients, drop a bag of flour on the floor, or overcook an egg because we are looking for where we put the salt.

In programming, screen real estate has precisely the same value. When we have only a single monitor to view our work, we have to make compromises. There's not enough room to keep our development environments, browsers, and communication clients "on the countertop" at the same time. We're forced to flip between states 1,000 times during the course of a workday.

Suppose we want to rigorously test our code in a development environment while running the compiled application in a browser. Without enough screen real estate, we can see only one application at once—or maybe both applications resized to thin, horizontally scrolling widgets. Those little adjustments are distracting. They can kill a tenuous train of thought.

Just like the kitchen countertop, multiple monitors are a big boon to productivity.

In a dual-monitor setup, keep your programming environment in the full screen directly in front of you. In the other screen, keep up your test browser and have any other programs (such as email or chat clients) accessible from there as well. This way, you can stay focused on your development and test on another screen at all times.

If you have a triple-monitor setup, keep your programming environment directly in front of you, your test browser up on one screen, and all the other programs (such as email or chat clients) on a third. If you want to concentrate for a few minutes without the distractions of blinking taskbar icons and unread messages, you can just turn off the third screen temporarily.

As an aside, the next time you're out on a job hunt, looking for that next great gig, scan the office to quickly tell whether management is in touch with their development team—whether they really care about the work environment they've set up for their developers. Count the number of monitors in the room and divide by the number of employees. This number is your *in-touch* quotient.

In-Touch Quotient	Diagnosis
1	Not in touch.
1 to <2	Somewhat in touch.
2 to <3	Very in touch.
More than 3	You're actually in a day-trader's office. Leave *immediately*.

The environment you've been running on for a few years may seem fine to you right now, and you might be accustomed to its temperaments. But spending those extra few thousands of dollars is an *investment in productivity*, not just an expenditure.

Essay 22

Keep a Personal To-Do List

It's amazing how sometimes the simplest tool can make us substantially more productive. Enter the personal to-do list.

A personal to-do list is *not*—I repeat, *not*—like a project timeline or a Gantt chart. Those documents serve a group. They are too sweeping for a single person. They make projections about the broad scope of a project rather than lay the path for the next couple of paces ahead of us. While they are useful "big-picture" documents, they don't help us get organized.

A personal to-do list is also *not* an overflowing email inbox. Using our emails to remind us of things we have to do is futile. Email is a smorgasbord of fragmented conversations and questions interspersed with unprioritized tasks, not a clearly defined list of things to do right now. Email isn't made for quick scanning.

A personal to-do list is *just a checklist*. Nothing more, nothing less. It's quick and simple yet deceptively powerful.

When you receive a task in your inbox, write the task down in your personal to-do list. When you've adjusted your timeline to accommodate a must-have feature, break down that feature into small to-dos on your personal to-do list.

At first glance, the personal to-do list seems like just another thing to manage; all the items in it likely originated from some other document. That smells like bad practice because it violates the "don't repeat yourself" mantra most of us follow in our code. However, a personal to-do list is a rare occasion where duplication is *OK*. That's because it doesn't serve the same purpose as other, more rigid documents.

Unlike other documents, to-do lists are made for constant adjustment. They are never set in stone. To-dos are added, checked off, pushed back, pushed up, and thrown out daily. Unlike project timelines and Gantt charts, a personal to-do list doesn't care about the past. Its starting point is always right now. It also doesn't guess at things. It's full of organized, real tasks that have to get finished in the very near future.

The Ingredients of a Good Personal To-Do List

A personal to-do list for programmers ought to have the following qualities:

- It is one, and only one, list.

- It has four buckets: Today, Tomorrow, Two days from now, and Future.

- It isn't a nested set of dependencies. Each to-do lives directly under one of the buckets mentioned earlier.

- It's easily modifiable. You can move items up and down the list easily.

- It is composed of short tasks that take no more than a couple of hours to complete. Items in the Future bucket can be broader. We'll get to that later.

- It's online. You have access to it wherever you're working.

I use Ta-da List from 37signals because it's simple and free. Here's how you set up a personal to-do list using Ta-da List.

Create a new list, and then add the four divider items. Since you can't make dividers in Ta-da List, just make four to-do items that you'll never actually check off. Put dashes before and after the label so it's easier to differentiate them from the other, real to-dos.

My Personal To-Do List

- --- TODAY ---
- --- TOMORROW ---
- --- TWO DAYS FROM NOW ---
- --- FUTURE ---

Add another item

As you start adding to-dos, put them under their appropriate divider. If it's something you absolutely need to finish today, drag it under TODAY. If it's something you need to get done tomorrow, drag it under TOMORROW. If it's just further out, put it under TWO DAYS FROM NOW. If you're not sure exactly when but know there's a task coming up pretty soon, drag it under FUTURE.

Because nothing about a to-do list is final, if you're unsure whether to put something under TOMORROW vs. TWO DAYS FROM NOW, lean toward the closer date. If you finish tomorrow and it still hasn't become top priority, you can leave it for the next day.

Breaking Down Features into To-Dos

Any to-dos you bring under TODAY, TOMORROW, or TWO DAYS FROM NOW should be small tasks (no more than a couple of hours). For instance, Build registration and login is a bad to-do. Too much time goes by before you're able to see progress on your to-do list. Instead, Build registration and login might be added as a series of these bite-size tasks:

My Personal To-Do List

- ▢ --- TODAY ---
- ▢ Registration: Build HTML form
- ▢ Registration: Implement JS validation
- ▢ Registration: Verify email uniqueness
- ▢ Registration: Send email confirmation
- ▢ --- TOMORROW ---
- ▢ Login: Build login form
- ▢ Login: Implement JS validation
- ▢ --- TWO DAYS FROM NOW ---
- ▢ Login: Build "Forgot password" form
- ▢ Login: Build "Forgot password" email
- ▢ Login: Build "Reset password" form
- ▢ Login: Build "Reset password" confirmation
- ▢ --- FUTURE ---
- ▢ Something down the road...

Add another item

Here, we've broken down building a registration component into a three-day, ten-task to-do list. It's organized without seeming overly complex.

Each to-do is a small chunk of work. Once we finish one thing, we can check it off. It gives us instant gratification each time we *finish* something. Instead of waiting until we complete an entire component, we see progress frequently as we go.

At the end of the day, we may not get to everything we had in mind. Oftentimes, we'll have an item or two that didn't make it. By sundown, our to-do list often looks like this, with something still remaining for today:

My Personal To-Do List

- ▢ --- TODAY ---
- ▢ Registration: Send email confirmation
- ▢ --- TOMORROW ---
- ▢ Login: Build login form
- ▢ Login: Implement JS validation
- ▢ --- TWO DAYS FROM NOW ---
- ▢ Login: Build "Forgot password" form
- ▢ Login: Build "Forgot password" email
- ▢ Login: Build "Reset password" form
- ▢ Login: Build "Reset password" confirmation
- ▢ --- FUTURE ---
- ▢ Something down the road...

Add another item

- ☑ Registration: Verify email uniqueness
- ☑ Registration: Implement JS validation
- ☑ Registration: Build HTML form

How Tomorrow Becomes Today

So, what happens when tomorrow comes around? What if there was an item or two we didn't get to yesterday? It takes just a few seconds to get our to-do list updated again. In Ta-da List, it's two simple mouse drags.

First, drag the TOMORROW divider just above the TWO DAYS FROM NOW divider. Everything that was set for tomorrow now falls under TODAY. Anything we *didn't* get to yesterday still remains in TODAY. Drag TWO DAYS FROM NOW just above the FUTURE divider. Everything that was set for two days out now falls under TOMORROW.

Back to the Future

Each day, glance at your growing list of FUTURE items. If you'll need to finish one of those items in the next two days, break that task down into bite-size tasks, and move them appropriately.

My Personal To-Do List

- ☐ --- TODAY ---
- ☐ Registration: Send email confirmation
- ☐ Login: Build login form
- ☐ Login: Implement JS validation
- ☐ --- TOMORROW ---
- ☐ Login: Build "Forgot password" form
- ☐ Login: Build "Forgot password" email
- ☐ Login: Build "Reset password" form
- ☐ Login: Build "Reset password" confirmation
- ☐ --- TWO DAYS FROM NOW ---
- ☐ --- FUTURE ---
- ☐ Something down the road...

Add another item

- ☑ Registration: Verify email uniqueness
- ☑ Registration: Implement JS validation
- ☑ Registration: Build HTML form

Reevaluating What Matters Each Day

A personal to-do list is perfectly made for adjustments to priority. It rolls with the daily uncertainty of software development. Perhaps an item that's destined to be done today doesn't seem as important anymore. Just drag it into the TOMORROW bucket or even further down. Similarly, an item set for TWO DAYS FROM NOW may be something you have the energy for today. Move it, finish it, and check it off.

There will be many days when we won't get to all of our TODAY items. We may have an item stuck on TODAY for days on end because other priorities get in the way.

But after a while, patterns begin to emerge. Certain to-dos always seem to linger around our TODAY bucket or routinely get pushed back to TOMORROW. These "bad egg" to-dos might not be as important as we thought when we first added them. When a to-do item hangs around for a week or two, just get rid of it. Avoiding unimportant work is just as productive as completing important work.

"Well, no wonder! I had it on my *not* to-do list!"

A personal to-do list is not black magic; it will not do the work for us. Still, it helps us organize and adjust simultaneously while seeing real progress every day. Feeling good about each day's small bit of progress keeps us on track to stay productive tomorrow.

Essay 23

Create "Off-Time" with Your Team

Productivity can happen only when there's time allowed to be productive. That's less obvious than it sounds. Basic events in everyday work—meetings, phone calls, shoulder tapping—are so commonplace now that we forget these are all *distractions*.

How have some companies solved the distraction issue?

37signals preaches a philosophy of staying away from their employees. In *Rework* [FH10], they mention how interruption not only stops us from working on the thing we're working on but breaks us out of our natural "alone zone"—that state of completely concentrating on our work.

Google is well known for its "20 percent rule," which allows engineers one day a week to work exclusively on a company-related project they're particularly passionate about.[4] Many of these side projects turned into some of Google's best known products, like Google News and Gmail.

Companies that want their employees to thrive, not just survive, need ways of allowing that to *actually* happen.

If I had my druthers, I'd work from home every day. Extracting myself from the nagging feeling that there's a client call looming or that someone needs my help on something *right now* is a huge burden lifted. I can just focus on my code all day.

But we also serve clients who sometimes need lots of attention. We rarely have the luxury of spending full days on pure programming. There will always be fires to fight, clients to call, and emails to answer.

Welcome, Off-Time

A few years ago, I instated off-time at my company. It's a way of mimicking the *get-out-of-my-face-and-just-let-me-work* rules that other companies implement, while still catering to our clients' needs (aka calls, emails, and general attentiveness). Here's how it works.

We have two-hour shifts of off-time for each developer, every day. When you're on off-time...

- No emails need to be answered.
- No meetings. You are unavailable during this time.
- No phone calls.
- No co-worker instant messages you.
- No co-worker talks to you.

During off-time, we place a white flag on our desks. After two hours off, we go back to checking email and responding to phone calls and instant messages. Then, we proceed as normal. The golden rule is simple: don't bug the person on off-time.

It would be great to have company-wide off-time, but it's unreasonable for our business. It means we would essentially shut down from any client or internal communication for

---

4.   http://www.nytimes.com/2007/10/21/jobs/21pre.html

two hours. That's just too long for some of our clients, especially when we're in the midst of a release.

We remedy this by setting up staggered shifts. They look something like this:

- *Shift 1*: 10 a.m. to noon daily—Ka Wai, Michael
- *Shift 2*: 2 p.m. to 4 p.m. daily—Anthony, Mustafa
- *Shift 3*: 4 p.m. to 6 p.m. daily—Tom, Craig

Because shifts are staggered, only one or two people are off at any given time. The company doesn't just shut down; for the most part, we're available.

Someone Else Can Help You

For us, who goes on off-time isn't random. We pair up members in generally different roles for each off-time shift. I tend to work closest with Mustafa, Tom with Mike, and Anthony with Craig. So, we don't share the same off-time.

That means if there's an urgent issue, a natural counterpart is available to discuss it. If Craig has a question for me at 11:30 a.m., he can ask Mustafa instead. If I have a question for Tom at 4:30 p.m., I can ask Michael. If a client sets up a phone meeting for someone during his off-time, there's a natural counterpart who will be available at that time instead.

Interruption as the Last Resort

Since off-time cuts us off from the person on it, it also makes everyone think harder about their own problems. We're more prone to ask, "Is this something I can solve with a little Googling instead of bothering someone?" Interruption is the last resort.

Off-time gives each of us ten hours of interruption-free time a week, with almost no disruption to our availability to clients and ourselves. It's a great way to sustain productivity in a realistic way.

So, whether it's off-time, a free day to do your own thing, or staying physically away from each other, think of how you can make yourself more productive by leaving one another alone.

Essay 24

Work in Small, Autonomous Teams

Many big companies tout the now overly clichéd line "People are our greatest asset." It's nauseating. Many of these same companies identify employees with a badge number, give away gift cards as temporary lifelines to an employee's quickly fading motivation, and consequently see huge turnover rates. No big deal.

Some companies, especially very large ones, can hire and hire again, replacing a part for another part, to keep the engine churning. They can continue to sign big contracts with other big companies and squeeze all the youthful exuberance out of their new employees for a good year. Once they've rung them dry, it's off to the market once again. More hires, more replacements, more of the same just-good-enough work to keep the ship afloat.

We often look at this corporate phenomena as a result of "big business." It's red tape. It's bureaucracy. It's meetings. It's indecision begetting indecision. Yet, all the while, they continue to toe the corporate line: people are their greatest asset.

Truth be told, in my small consultancy, people *aren't* our greatest asset. I know full well there are (many) better pro-grammers, designers, thinkers, and writers out there than me. Not one of us is the best at our job. Somebody out there is better.

But what makes us productive is the working relationships that form over time. I've sweated, year after year, with nearly the same group of like-minded workers. That sense of familiarity we have within our team means we know how each person likes to work.

Some of us like to work deliberately, cautiously thinking through each line of code. Others like to take big swings, leave a mess, and clean up afterward. Some of us need to work alone longer and fight through a problem solo, while others need more collaboration up front. Over time, each of us complements each other in a different way. We adapt to the people around us. Over time, we start to gel—in the truest sense of the word.

At the same time, that familiarity lets us argue without worrying about hurting each other's feelings. There is no "feeling each other out" when you've been in the trenches with the same army for years. We can fight full-fledged for an idea we believe in without the debilitating worry of hurt feelings. Our meetings are active, engaging, and sometimes heated. We get issues ironed out and come to a resolution. Compare that to the average corporate meeting full of questions and noncommittal answers. In those meetings, avoiding confrontation seems to trump getting to the best answer.

That's why I advocate that the best environment for programmers is within small, autonomous teams that have very low turnover. You can still find them inside of big corporations, but they're much easier to spot inside small shops. In today's landscape, small shops are the ones sprouting out big things, because they can get to decisions quicker, research and learn without the hindrances of corporate red tape, and ultimately build faster. Think of all the hugely successful software used by the masses yet produced by very small organizations. Here's just a small sliver of them:

- *Campaign Monitor*: Email marketing software for web designers

- *Litmus*: Email previews and monitoring

- *GitHub*: Version control repository for software development projects

- *Braintree*: Online payment gateway for SaaS services

- *Basecamp*: Project management and collaboration software

- *Angry Birds*: Mobile puzzle video game

Their collective familiarity turns a group of pretty good individuals into a singular, great team, producing amazing products.

Eliminate the "We" in Productivity

In productive team development, clarity is king. Yes, knowing who is responsible for which piece of the puzzle is critical. But it's just as important to know who *isn't* going to be responsible for that piece as well. They have other pieces to handle.

When you're communicating with your co-workers or your clients, particularly in meetings and over email, get out of the habit of using the word "we." Instead, say exactly *who*.

Observe how often you're using the word "we" the next time you're in a technical meeting. When you say "we," you're probably really saying "some of us," "just a few of us," or oftentimes even just you (or John or Mary). Rarely does your "we" actually mean the collective whole.

"OK, now that we all agree, let's all go back to
our desks and discuss why this won't work."

But that's the impression that using the "w" word creates. It suddenly throws the blanket of responsibility, unnecessarily, over everyone. It blurs the line between who really should be concerned about a problem and those who should be focusing on other tasks. More importantly, it hides who you should really talk to if you want to provide feedback.

For instance, if you're writing a tool to transfer data off a legacy database and need to know what the schema looks like for the Customers table, you don't need to consult with the entire company. A front-end designer probably doesn't know or care. Even if the database is managed by a team of people, find the exact person who's responsible for getting you what you need. Don't say that we need to get the schema; say exactly *who* needs to get that information to you.

If you don't know who, then *pick someone*. They'll either get you what you need or delegate that responsibility to the right person. Specifying responsibility directly gets things moving in one direction: forward.

And that's just the opposite of what the "we" mentality condones. "We" turns into fifteen people listening in on a phone call, twelve recipients copied on an email, or a roundtable of people writing notes about things they don't understand or don't really matter to them. "We" just turns into a big cloud of talk when only a few people really understand the language being spoken. "We" makes things exponentially noisier than they need to be.

"We" Feeds the Noise Virus

The problem isn't just that it causes more noise; "we" is also the ammo that prolongs and multiplies noise. When you let "we" into the conversation, you're inviting the talk to get even bigger and bigger over time.

Why? "We" lets you ask questions that don't have to be answered immediately. They often sound rhetorical. It opens up new, often uncritical, avenues of conversation that get away from the question you were trying to answer from the get-go.

- What do "we" think about this feature addition?

- Do "we" need to add more hardware to our web server? Can "we" get some performance metrics?

- What can "we" do to make this user experience better?

These questions are often asked at the end of a meeting as the setup for another meeting. Even if it's just one or two people really making the decision, everyone will agree that "we need to think more about this." These questions appear perfectly normal to ask during a group meeting or within an email. But switch "we" for real humans—those warm-blooded mammals all around you—and suddenly those rhetorical questions turn direct.

- What does Jennifer think about this feature addition?

- Does Mike need to add more hardware to our web server? Can Anthony get us some performance metrics?

- What can Tom do to make this user experience better?

When you direct the questions at someone, people get moving.

The Bystander Effect

"We"-type questions often sputter because it's human nature. It's no different from the bystander effect: a person in an emergency situation is likely to get help faster from a lone bystander than from any single person within a large group of bystanders.

> According to a basic principle of social influence, bystanders monitor the reactions of other people in an emergency situation to see whether others think it is necessary to intervene. Since everyone is doing exactly the same thing (nothing), they all conclude from the inaction of others that help is not needed.[5]

When more people are put into a situation, there's less of a chance that any one of them will do anything to resolve it. Instead, pinpoint the exact people responsible for the task.

As simple as it may sound, swapping "we" for direct names (or even "I") makes a huge difference in team productivity. In meetings, in emails, or over the phone, using "we" slows down momentum, leaving your team less aware of who should do what *and* who shouldn't do what. "We" is the verbal high-fructose corn syrup of productivity. It might sound sweet, but it's loaded with a whole load of fluff that's just not good for you.

---

5.   http://en.wikipedia.org/wiki/Bystander_effect

As we've seen in the last few essays, sometimes productivity is simply about reducing complexity: working with fewer people, delegating responsibility to a single person, or eliminating the external noise of team development. In the next chapter, we'll focus on complexity in our software.

CHAPTER 5

Complexity

Aside from death and taxes, complexity may be the only other sure bet in life. Complexity always grows over time. In our industry, it's the unavoidable consequence of maturing software. Unless we're willing to remove features from an application, there is simply no way to sidestep it.

"What the heck is that supposed to mean?!"

If we can't get rid of complexity, our next job is to stifle its growth. We need to recognize when complexity *isn't* necessary and develop a finely tuned nose for it. If we know what it smells like and if we can pick up the all-too-familiar stench from every nook and cranny of our software, we'll be better off in the end.

Essay 26

Sniff Out Bad Complexity

Bad complexity is complexity that just *doesn't have to be there.*

That's not always easy to spot. Sometimes even the pieces we think have to be there really don't. This happened even to Thomas Jefferson.

In 1776, Jefferson sat on the committee that drafted the Declaration of Independence. The committee gave him the privilege of writing the first draft. When the draft was completed, he sent it to his friend, Benjamin Franklin, for review. Franklin returned the draft with much of Jefferson's clever language erased.

Jefferson was none too happy, but Franklin tried to convince his friend why this was for the better. Franklin told him this story:

> When I was a journeyman printer, one of my companions, an apprentice hatter, having served out his time, was about to open shop for himself.
>
> His first concern was to have a handsome signboard, with a proper inscription. He composed it in these words:
>
> *"John Thompson, Hatter, makes and sells hats for ready money"*
>
> with a figure of a hat subjoined; but he thought he would submit it to his friends for their amendments.
>
> The first he showed it to thought the word "Hatter" tautologous, because it was followed by the words "makes hats," which showed he was a hatter. It was struck out.
>
> The next observed that the word "makes" might as well be omitted, because his customers would not care who made the hats. If good and to their mind, they would buy them, by whomsoever made. He struck it out.
>
> A third said he thought the words "for ready money" were useless, because it was not the custom of the place to sell on credit. Everyone who purchased expected to pay. They were

parted with, and the inscription now stood, "John Thompson sells hats."

"Sells hats!" says the next friend. "Why, nobody will expect you to give them away. What then is the use of that word?" It was stricken out, and "hats" followed it, as there was one painted on the board.

So, the inscription was reduced ultimately to "John Thompson," with the figure of a hat subjoined.[1]

Plenty of software could take a cue from the hatter's sign. Does this button need to be there? Is this line of copy adding anything of value, or is it merely repeating something else that's already there? Does this new feature actually help make the task easier?

Consider what you could possibly remove from your software and still have it function the same.

Essay 27

The Simplicity Paradox

What makes complexity a strange phenomenon is this: *Everyone. Loves. Simple.* That's why people say "I just want things to be simple." Who says "I just want things to be complicated"...*ever*?

I decided to find out. So, I looked it up on Google.

As of this writing, if you Google the phrase "I want things to be simple," you'll get approximately 954,000 matching results. There is *one* unique matching results for the phrase "I want things to be complicated."

One. The only unique matching result? A blog post that I wrote about this very subject in October 2009. Extract myself from the annals of recorded human civilization, and apparently no one has ever wanted or even thought about the idea of voluntary complication.

---

1. http://www.pbs.org/benfranklin/l3_citizen_founding.html

Then, why do we run into this Jeffersonian problem of complexity when we're building our own stuff? Why do the things we produce often wind up festered in complication? How do so many well-intentioned pieces of software matriculate from simple idea to functional nightmare?

Simple Products Can Actually Be Hard to Build

Most ideas, simple at the surface, are viciously complicated when we get into the details. Ideas, at a high level, are always simple. Every business idea must be accompanied by the elevator pitch: sixty seconds to get the message across from beginning to end. We can't pack complexity into a sixty-second description.

When ideas start feeling complex, we leave the comforts of Idea Land and enter the naked reality of implementation. Once we dig into the details, we discover where all the holes in logic are. That's just the nature of *detail*. An idea that hasn't been thought through completely (read: most of them) has little chance of surviving Complexityville at this point. Rather than rethinking the idea altogether, it's sometimes easier to plow through the problems with head down and blinders up. Half-baked decisions are made, and features are added all for the sake of preserving the sanctity of the "big idea." Then, complexity festers.

Simple Sometimes Seems Like *Not Enough*

If everyone likes simple software and most software isn't simple to build, it would appear that the sweet spot for good software would be *both* simple to use *and* simple to build. It's a win-win for both user and developer. But that kind of software rarely exists in our world. There has to be something more to this mystery.

The answer lies in our own fear of inadequacy. When we build something simply, it doesn't feel like...*enough*. We convince ourselves into believing our customer isn't getting his money's worth. A simple thing that's *also* simple to build feels valueless. An idea that's easily implemented is rarely considered a "big idea" at all.

Venture capitalists don't throw millions of dollars at simple ideas. They throw all that money at the Donald Trump-esque superlatives. Is it best-in-class? Is it innovative? Is it cutting-edge? Oftentimes, these are just other ways of saying an idea is *complex* enough to be worth its weight.

Herein lies the paradox. From a builder's point of view, we often equate the worth of software we build to its complexity, and more complexity equals more value.

The view from the other side of the mirror is different. The reality is 90 percent of our users use only 10 percent of the features built in the average enterprise-level software. When users can't find the few functions they need because they're buried among the many features they don't need, they either take it out on their own perceived shortcomings or blame it on the software itself. While builders and stakeholders see simplicity as the shortcoming, users see complexity as the shortcoming.

At my company, the natural urge to complicate is something we resist constantly. We have to re-sell and re-pitch simple to ourselves all the time.

Countless internal arguments about features in our own software end up with incredibly simple solutions. Sometimes the UI just needs a small tweak in text. Other times, it's just a re-organization of links. Sometimes we'll argue for hours about a new feature before ultimately deciding the feature just isn't worth the complexity it adds.

The lesson is this. You don't have to "merit" lengthy hours of feature discussion with an equally large amount of feature additions. It's natural to feel that the amount of time you spend on something should parallel the amount of measurable output you put into the product, regardless of the benefit of that new feature. But free yourself from that debilitating thought. Once you've let go of the vulnerable feeling that simplicity cheapens your worth, you can finally get on with building good software.

A simple solution shouldn't be thought of as "not enough" of anything. Sometimes it is exactly enough of everything.

Complexity as a Game of Pickup Sticks

Pickup sticks is an old children's game where you try to remove individual plastic sticks from a pile without disturbing the others. You start the game by holding a bundle of sticks in your hand and letting them go. Most of the sticks fall in a pile in the middle, while a select few roll away from the center.

The object is to remove as many sticks as you can from the pile, one at a time, without disturbing the other sticks. You lose your turn if any other sticks in the pile are disturbed.

Maintaining complex software sometimes feels a lot like this game. Each stick represents a feature or function. Sometimes a feature can live outside and completely away from the others. Other times it affects a few components. And still other times it's completely intertwined with many other features.

Implementing a new feature is like adding a few new sticks into the mix. At a certain point, trying to remove any stick without disturbing the rest is nearly impossible. Complexity adds up fast.

As developers, we try our best to circumvent this by following good habits: encapsulating our code, scoping variables at the right level, breaking apart larger pieces of logic into bite-size chunks, or introducing patterns. It's our valiant attempt to align all of our sticks in parallel, side by side, so they don't touch each other. But consistently refactoring code into the "right" places while continuing to add more sticks into the mix can get hairy. It's easy to let our guard down.

Every time we add a new feature, we stand the chance of disrupting a host of other features that might not, at first, seem directly connected. As we add more features, those disruption points grow pretty rapidly.

Keep Complexity Under the Surface

"An extraordinarily complex mess."

That's what Nina Olson, the national Taxpayer Advocate for the U.S. Internal Revenue Service, calls the American tax system. The official book weighs in at about 6,500 pages. Can you imagine? If you think I'm lying, you're right. It's actually about *65,000* pages long.

This is why I absolutely love TurboTax, one of the most popular income tax preparation software packages in the United States. It has taken these 65,000 pages of documentation and miraculously curated some sort of usable software out of it for commoners like me. TurboTax could so easily have just reproduced the federal and state 1040 forms digitally, turning each line item into a text field and calculating a few fields here and there, and submitted the form via the Information Superhighway and be done with it.

It probably still would have a lot of fans.

Instead, TurboTax is like a personal tax wizard who understands that no one really wants to hang out with it. "Get your W-2 out and copy the numbers into me." "Do you own a farm? No?! Then let's not ever mention it again." It even knows when it's asking me esoteric questions, by letting me know that something is very unlikely or uncommon—"This probably doesn't apply to you."

TurboTax has done a heroic job of making tax filing at least palatable. I can only imagine what a stinky mess the underlying code must be. Logic must exist not just for federal law but for each of the fifty states and for each of the thousands of local counties and beyond. And within those parameters, there's code for single and married people, small-business owners, investors, students, philanthropists, first-time home buyers, the unemployed, the just-retired, the forgetful, the poor, the rich, the richer, and—yes, farmers.

Couple that with the annual changes to tax laws; every little rule taken out or put in to account for some earmark in government spending that make up those 65,000 pages of dead trees. If you think you're angry about a couple extra hundred dollars you owe the government, imagine being a TurboTax developer who has to write yet another weird bit of conditional logic for someone who's just bought an environmentally friendly motorboat in Mississippi within the last six months.

Is any of that code even worth refactoring? What would they refactor when the very code they're writing today might be obsolete after the next Congressional recess or might depend on a totally different set of parameters down the road?

TurboTax is proof that, even when the task at hand is an *extraordinarily complex mess*, the software doesn't have to be. You can squeeze all that complexity underneath the surface, interpret that mess into some reasonably digestible set of usable functions, and create some really helpful and far more simplistic software.

Essay 30

"Hard to Code" Might Mean "Hard to Use"

TurboTax takes something nearly impossible to comprehend and makes it approachable to the masses. Complexity is shifted from the user to the code.

However, not always is this shift a zero-sum game. Sometimes overly complex logic is just a sign that the function of the application is confusing. Complex code supporting a complex interface? How about we don't?

Confusion in the Elevator

Imagine we're part of a team of engineers attempting to build better software to control an elevator for a 50-story high-rise. The elevator can monitor which floor people enter and which floor button they press. Our manager walks in with one simple commandment: people are complaining about waiting inside the elevator, so let's build the elevator so that people collectively spend the least amount of time in it.

"No, I must have missed that."

We start brainstorming through the scenarios. Suppose John steps in from the ground floor and pushes the button to go to his penthouse on floor 50. On its way up, the elevator stops at floor 8. In comes Steve, the UPS delivery guy, with a large brown box. He has to deliver the package to someone on floor 5, so he quickly presses 5.

What should the elevator do? Should the elevator stop at floor 5 first because it's closer or stop at floor 5 second because it's already heading up?

If the elevator heads back down to floor 5, John and Steve will pass a total of 59 floors. John will have gone up eight floors, back down three, and then back up the remaining forty-five floors to his penthouse. Steve will have gone down only three floors.

- John: 8 up + 3 down + 45 up = 56 floors passed.
- Steve: 3 down = 3 floors passed.
- Total floors spent by John and Steve: *59*.

Compare this to the alternative. If the elevator, instead, keeps going up, before coming back down to floor 5, they'd collectively pass more than twice that many:

- John: 50 up = 50 floors passed.
- Steve: 42 up + 45 down = 87 floors passed.
- Total floors spent by John and Steve: *137*.

The answer is clear. The elevator should go down to drop Steve and his brown box off first before going all the way to Steve's penthouse. We all agree the new elevator is going to be all the rage!

Let's continue our brainstorm. Suppose Steve, the UPS delivery guy, had entered the elevator at floor 30, instead of floor 8. Here's what happens if the elevator comes back down first:

- John: 30 up + 25 down + 45 up = 100 floors passed.
- Steve: 25 down = 25 floors passed.
- Total floors spent by John and Steve: *125*.

Now, what if, instead, the elevator kept going up to John's penthouse before coming back down?

- John: 50 up = 50 floors passed.
- Steve: 20 up + 45 down = 65 floors passed.
- Total floors spent by John and Steve: *115*.

In this scenario, we save 10 "man" floors if the elevator goes up! So, depending on when Steve gets on, the elevator may decide to continue its ascent or descend first before re-ascending. With two people, programming for the optimal elevator ride for two people is a fairly benign task.

Now suppose a third person, Samantha, enters the elevator. Now, there are six potential ways we could let each person off the elevator. Our program would have to calculate the total number of floors passed for each scenario before deciding on the best route.

- Case 1: John, Steve, Samantha
- Case 2: John, Samantha, Steve
- Case 3: Steve, John, Samantha
- Case 4: Steve, Samantha, John
- Case 5: Samantha, Steve, John
- Case 6: Samantha, John, Steve

In fact, the number of scenarios that need to be tested is just the factorial of the number of people on the elevator at a given time:

- 2 people = 2! = 2 comparisons
- 3 people = 3! = 6 comparisons
- 4 people = 4! = 24 comparisons
- 8 people = 8! = 40,320 comparisons

Once we get past just a few people, the number of cases to test becomes impractical. But that's only *one* aspect of the complexity problem.

People are getting on and off the elevator at different times. Each time a new person enters the elevator, we would need to track how many floors the existing passengers have already passed before making a new set of calculations.

In other words, we couldn't sufficiently deduce the path the elevator has already taken just by looking at who's currently on it. If Mike enters on floor 25 and then Sanjay enters at floor 35, did the elevator travel ten floors between Mike's entrance and Sanjay's, or did it go back to floor 21 first to drop off Samantha?

At more than two elevator riders, we'd *also* need to track when people leave the elevator so we can omit them from future calculations.

In addition, what happens when someone forgets to hit their floor number or hits the wrong floor number and then presses a button during mid-ascent? Does our software recalculate and potentially shift gears in mid-flight?

If you're new to programming, this is, sadly, not an exaggeration of how complex a seemingly simple goal—such as getting people off an elevator as quickly as possible—can be.

Complexity with Little Payoff

After all those extra obstacles, suppose, somehow, that we've built the perfect system. We've managed to write code in such a way that everyone collectively leaves the elevator in the shortest amount of time—calculating thousands of scenarios in a split second, taking into account everyone's already taken path. It's a true feat of technology! But how are John, Steve, and the rest of the gang faring? Probably not so well.

Code is great at processing the tediously automatable, and this is certainly a case of the extraordinarily tedious. But humans aren't good at it. Nobody inside the elevator can possibly run through all the scenarios in their heads that quickly. The people waiting to get off are at the complete mercy of the elevator, not knowing which general direction they'll be going when the next person gets on, nor why.

Here we have a case where *hard to code means hard to use*. Complexity, in this case, hurts *both* ways. By the time even a fourth person gets on the elevator, there are just too many scenarios for a human to know what route the elevator wants to take. Even when the elevator is accomplishing the goal of getting everyone off in the fewest amount of collectively traveled floors, the people inside are left wondering when it'll be their turn.

They might well prefer the simple, traditional algorithm an elevator abides by.

Sure, they probably wouldn't reach the optimal path, but by favoring a simpler solution, the people in the elevator have better knowledge of what's going on. That level of predictability trumps the more complex solution even if it's theoretically more efficient.

When details become egregiously hard to code, it *may* be a smell that the actual function of the system is difficult to understand. And while you may pat yourself on the back for successfully programming something really complex, others are punching you *in* the back after they use it.

Essay 31

Know When to Refactor

Another smell of complexity arises when we think too far ahead in our code. There's a price to pay for being too cute or too cerebral about the actual thing we're trying to build. A classic case is implementing a design pattern too early.

Don't get me wrong, design patterns are wonderful things. When a common programming approach happens over and over again, we get excited. We've all experienced that sense that our code could be doing something *greater* than just solving the concrete task at hand.

When we've had this feeling a few times and successfully refactored our code into more abstract patterns, it's easy to feel invincible. We work like a crime dog, sniffing out any small sign or clue, any hint, that another abstraction lives above our straightforward piece of code.

But very quickly, our sixth sense can come back to bite us where it really hurts. Most of us have heard, or experienced, the horror stories of "architecting yourself into a corner." It's where we've taken an abstract approach to solving a problem way too far.

The Danger of Refactoring Too Soon

For example, suppose you're working on an intranet for Burgeoning Web Company. They're small, and they have only two departments: IT and sales. The executives at Burgeoning Web Company want the ability to calculate anticipated bonuses for their employees based on a bunch of employee parameters. But each department wants to base bonuses on different measurements.

The IT department only wants to give bonuses to employees as a percentage of their current salary and only to those who have stuck around for five years. The sales department wants to give everyone a $1,000 base bonus, plus a standard $500 incremental bonus for each year they've worked at Burgeoning Web Company. After all, the company is burgeoning, and the execs are generous folks.

You start coding. You've built an Employee class that will contain all the information you need to calculate an employee's bonus. You then write a simple function, which, for now, contains one simple conditional statement to return a given employee's anticipated bonus.

```
public decimal GetBonusForEmployee(Employee employee)
{
  if (employee.department == Departments.IT)
  {
    // Calculate bonus the "IT" way
    if (employee.Years >= 5)
    {
      return .1 * employee.Salary;
    }

    return 0;
  }
  else
  {
    // Calculate bonus the "Sales" way
    return 1000 + 500 * employee.Years;
  }
}
```

You write a little tool to load all employees into a collection of Employee objects and then apply the previous method to each. Your work is done. Beer time.

But your mind begins to think about the other possibilities that lie ahead when Burgeoning Web Company really begins to burgeon. What do you do when the third or fourth department comes along? Swap the conditional logic for a switch statement! But why wait? Let's anticipate it now so you're ready for the future:

```
public decimal getBonusForEmployee(Employee employee)
{
  switch(employee.department)
  {
    case Departments.IT:

      // Calculate bonus the "IT" way
      if (employee.Years >= 5)
      {
        return .1 * employee.Salary;
      }

      return 0;

    case Departments.SALES:

      //Calculate bonus the "Sales" way
      return 1000 + 500 * employee.Years;
  }
}
```

Beautifully done! The switch statement is a safe anticipatory move. It explicitly identifies the sales department instead of relegating it to the else statement. When marketing comes along, you know just where it fits.

This small refactoring makes sense. Your code is now more explicit, and it's easier to scan. Another developer could come in and pick it up right away.

Sensing your higher calling, you decide to do more. What happens when two departments become....ten? In a few months, there could be new departments springing up, such as legal, production, accounting, and the janitorial staff. The switch statement will eventually get unwieldy. It will be tainted with complex calculations that have no business lying there, exposed so nakedly at the surface of the bonus calculation method.

You rifle through your favorite design patterns book (I highly recommend Joshua Kerievsky's *Refactoring to Patterns*

[Ker04]) and —*voilà*— the Strategy pattern! Move all those one-off bonus calculations into individual strategy classes (e.g., ITBonusCalculationStrategy and SalesBonusCalculationStrategy) that each implement a Bonus Calculation Strategy interface (IBonusCalculationStrategy). The interface will require each implementing class to define a CalculateBonus() method.

Once that's done, you modify the Employee class to contain a concrete strategy instance and create one new public method that will return an employee's bonus.

With the Strategy pattern, you can now remove the getBonus-ForEmployee() method altogether. The calculation of an employee's bonus can live in the class itself. So, all those nasty algorithms lie elegantly in the soft cushiony pillows of individual implementations of the IBonusCalculationStrategy interface.

Since you've gone this far, you decide to embellish your code. You abstract the creation of employees into a Factory pattern. This way, you can create department-specific employee creator classes to assign a corresponding bonus strategy for an employee.

You've completely removed the conditional switch on departments (it's taken care of in the employee creator classes) and the nasty calculation logic (it's buried in department-specific strategy classes). Wonderful!

Once department 15 comes along, this architecture will be a sight to see.

Weeks and months go by. The winter hits, and times are tough for Burgeoning Web Company. Still no new departments. Meanwhile, the bonus logic has changed. You go back in, stepping through code and wondering what happened to your once simple logic. Ah yes. It's been strategized and factoryized.

Another couple months go by. Burgeoning Web Company calls and says they've fired the sales team, and it'll just be the CEO working the phone with his team of developers. Wanting to keep developer morale, the CEO still wants to offer bonuses but now based solely on seniority.

It's time to shed a tear. You've placed all your bets on the department-specific bonus rules. It was, by all accounts, a safe bet one year ago. You've built the walls, ladders, and slides to account for every possible department bonus for the next one hundred years. The entire refactoring has gone to waste. It's not just over-architected clutter; it's spoiled clutter. You unearth your strategy classes, remove the factory methods, and submissively decide that a potentially nasty but quite all right conditional statement will do just fine for now.

Patterns are wonderful concepts. However, they should be implemented with the utmost caution. Anticipating logic in the future, more often than not, will lead to unintended complexity.

If there is a golden rule, it's that an application shouldn't be forced into a well-documented design pattern or set of patterns. Rather, a design pattern (or set of them) should be implemented as fully as needed to fit the desired tasks of the application and the most likely scenarios for the near future.

When you study a design pattern, read it as a general approach to solving a particular problem, not as a strict, rigid solution to a problem. Patterns all have pros and cons. While patterns make some tasks more elegant to perform, you always lose something else. Since most of today's web applications are constantly changing based on new customer or client requirements, finding the "perfect" set of patterns from the get-go is more dream than reality.

Does this mean we shouldn't anticipate for change at all? No. Problems manifest when we don't pay any attention to where our architecture is headed.

The Headache of Unmanageable Legacy Code

Examine any codebase whose authors decided not to make simple refactorings when they were necessary. The problems reveal themselves quickly. Variables are scoped at the wrong level or, even worse, accessible globally with some bizarre naming convention to ensure they'll always be unique. Conditional logic reads more like the terms on a Terms of

Use page: a bunch of unrelated truths stitched together with ands and ors that have collectively lost all meaning to the next unlucky soul who has to modify it.

We find this often in legacy code that's been handed down from generation to generation of developers that came into it without much passion and came out of it with even less. Method signatures become unruly, and method calls look like the code itself isn't sure what it's doing:

```
calculateBonusesForTeam(.02, 155000, null, 0, 0, null,
new Employee(), null, null, false, true);
```

Over time, unconsidered refactorings get expensive. Maintenance becomes asymptomatically slower. Forget big changes; even small changes, the ones we always take for granted, might collapse a codebase that's long since forgotten any basic set of good habits.

Let's get back to the Burgeoning Web Company story. At some point, refactoring the bonus calculations into a Strategy pattern might have made sense. Moving employee creation methods into a factory class might have been useful. *It just wasn't at the time.*

Over-architect too early in the development life cycle, and we're left with a hole waiting to be filled. Under-architect, and we're left without any option or motivation to evolve our software any further.

> "The hole and the patch should be commensurate." — Thomas Jefferson to James Madison

Perhaps Jefferson was channeling his conversation with Benjamin Franklin a few years earlier.

Anticipate, but anticipate cautiously. Whether it's just a small change or a large pattern shift, know what you're gaining and losing each time you decide to refactor.

Essay 32

Develop a Programming Cadence

So, how do we manage anticipating too early to change vs. reacting too late to change?

Consider software development like we're driving a stick shift. As we start, we're in first gear: coding away at a steady pace. The more we code, the less efficient we become. At some point, we have to shift up a gear.

Shifting up a gear, in programming terms, is cleaning up our code: taking a step back to refactor, abstract, or implement a pattern. It means taking the time to consider how to change our habits at a particular point in the development process. Doing this does not mean we've made a mistake. It's natural and necessary.

We have to shift in code just as we have to when we're driving. Still, if we do it too soon, we'll spend a lot of time trying to regain our speed. Do it too late (or not at all), and our code will burn out. Knowing when to shift is essential. It keeps the development process running as efficiently as possible. We don't shift just to shift; we have to do it when it's right. We have to find our programming cadence.

ANDERSON

"I was going so fast I figured it was better to keep my eyes on the road instead of the speedometer."

There is no set number of gears in software development. We can choose to have just 5 or 500 gears in our programming cadence. This depends on the complexity and scale of the project as well as our own willingness to shift gears. For more complex projects, allowing ourselves more gears means we can shift a lot more often. It means that if we shift a little too early, it won't take us too long to get back to speed. A little too late, and we haven't experienced too much burnout. For smaller ones, just a few gear shifts will do.

In the end, software complexity is necessary. It's the debt paid for more functionality. The key is to know when complexity feels right and when complexity feels wrong. Listen to your sixth sense when it tells you that, this time, complexity makes things worse on everyone. It's why what we do is much more art than it is science.

Complexity is one of those things we get better at understanding after years of being in the business. Veteran programmers are really good at managing it. Collectively, we need to pass this kind of wisdom onto future generations of passionate programmers. In the next chapter, we'll look at how we can become not just better programmers but better teachers.

CHAPTER 6

Teaching

One of the most difficult disciplines to master, in any field, is teaching. There are plenty of experts in the world but far fewer expert teachers.

Teaching isn't just *regurgitating* what we know. It's an art that requires us to step outside of our own heads and into the mind of someone who's learning something new. Simply knowing something is just one ingredient in the recipe for a successful teacher.

Too often, we expect someone with great knowledge to be an equally great teacher. But those qualities don't always come together. Isiah Thomas was a Hall of Fame point guard in the NBA. He was a 12-time NBA all-star and led the Detroit Pistons to two NBA World Championships as a player. Yet, as a head coach, he had a pedestrian record of 187 wins and 223 losses. Sometimes people with great knowledge and skill can't transfer those same traits to the people they're trying to mentor.

Teaching programming concepts to a relative newbie is even that much harder. There are no obvious indicators, like a win-loss record, to determine whether our instructions are getting through to our students.

For us, the road from a problem to a solution can be so complex that it's hard to even describe how we got to the final approach. But being able to do so is *critical*; it's the best way we can cultivate a future generation of passionate programmers.

In this chapter, we'll discuss both common behaviors to avoid and how to help others grasp all the complex knowledge we have in our heads.

Essay 33

Teaching Is Unlike Coding

At first, it seems like a great programmer should have all the skills to become a great teacher.

After all, coding has many of the same traits as teaching. Underneath all the fancy syntax, code is just a concrete set of instructions that tells a framework how to do something. Even if one microscopic detail is left out, we'll know soon enough. The compiler will yell at us.

Programs require us to code in a specific order too. We can't implement a concept before it has been defined yet, just like we couldn't teach someone how to multiply before they already understood how to add.

On the other hand, the act of coding isn't like teaching at all. In fact, it promotes bad habits that are entirely counterproductive to the art of teaching.

First, rarely do we code linearly. We don't start typing from the top of the page and work our way down to the end. We're incessantly jumping around our code, implementing functionality in an order that might not be obvious to the observer. It's especially true when we're finessing the smallest of details—a variable name change here or an erroneous data type there. If our coding process were anything like our teaching process, our lessons would be filled with stutters, misunderstandings, and take backs.

Second, coding lets us worry about the details of our stream of thought later. For instance, when I'm in the middle of, say, redefining the input parameters for a shared method, I make the change on the method's signature and then recompile. I *know* my code is not going to compile successfully. I expect a series of errors to pop up, each one complaining about a mismatched parameter type everywhere I'm calling that method. But I do this because it's a much faster way to see where I need to change everything else than scanning through code or doing a search on where the method is referenced.

Oftentimes, we compile our code not because we think our work is done but because we want to find out what we may have missed. A compiler is a lazy programmer's best friend. Ditto for unit tests, code hinting, and autocompletion.

All these niceties are essential for productive programming. They give us softly padded walls to bounce our code off of. They let us focus on the big concepts first and not worry too much about perfection in our code-speak. A good programming platform is simultaneously wiping our chin, correcting our grammar, and telling us what we really mean while we spew out semi-coherent lines of instruction. The faster and more efficient we are at coding, the more we rely on these tools to steer us in the right direction.

Teaching a newbie is entirely different. Every missed detail is a lost detail. We can't start our sentences expecting our student to finish them, at least not early on. And unlike a compiler, which invariably will forget our missteps once we correct them, people don't have as much luck separating the wrong details from the right. It may take us a dozen compiles before we finally get our code just right. But imagine the deer-in-headlights look on your students' faces if we were to correct ourselves that many times before our teaching lessons made complete sense.

The quirky ways we program efficiently run counter to the lockstep nature of teaching. You can't throw a bunch of concepts at someone, leave out a few of the details, and expect your human counterpart to know exactly what you *meant*. Instead of a list of errors and warnings, you'll be getting a blank stare.

A really good programmer doesn't automatically make a competent teacher.

Essay 34

Beware the "Curse of Knowledge"

In the popular Chip and Dan Heath book *Made to Stick: Why Some Ideas Survive and Others Die* [HH07], the brothers argue that once you've become an expert in a particular domain, it is nearly impossible to understand what it feels like to not understand that domain.

Think of how you would explain color to a person born without sight or how you would explain sound to a person born without hearing. In a less extreme example, think of a lawyer who can't give you a clear answer to a legal question without all sorts of abstractions and qualifications.

They call this the *curse of knowledge*.

"I think I speak for all of us when I say what in God's name are you talking about?"

Undoubtedly, one of the biggest abusers of the curse of knowledge is *us*.

Imagine we're explaining HTML to someone who has never worked with neither it nor any markup language. We start by talking about basic tags, like <p>, <br>, and <strong>. We then explain how content within tags inherits the properties of those tags and that each tag must be closed by adding the same tag with a forward slash inside of it.

After a bunch of head nodding, we move on to a simple bit of HTML:

```
<p>
  Hello world!
  <br />
  It's a <strong>beautiful day</strong>!
</p>
```

To us, there's not that much more to explain. It's a nice little paragraph with a break return inside of it and a couple words in bold. *Excellent!* It's time to speed forward to CSS and browser testing. Maybe we'll throw in some jQuery selector stuff before lunch!

Consider the vantage point from the eyes of the markup virgins. Here's what might be running through their minds:

- Why do we write the text inside of the <strong> tags inline when we don't do the same for <p>?

- Why does the <br> tag have a forward slash at the end instead of the beginning? Where is the counterpart that closes it?

- Can we put tags inside of the <strong> tag? What if we wrapped the word day with a <strong> tag? Does that make it...even stronger?

The HTML sample we gave to our student was fraught with small assumptions that we didn't even think could amount to any type of questioning. For someone new, every little nuance has to be picked apart. No assumptions, not even the fact that we write some tags inline and some tags with break returns for code readability, can be taken for granted.

So, when you're teaching a newbie, teach twice as slowly as you would want to. During each step, consider all the silent assumptions you're making and make it a point to explain those "obvious" things anyway. Ask your student, frequently, if things are making sense.

When you understand the *curse of knowledge* may be in full effect, you'll be more aware of the subtle details your student may be missing.

Teach with Obvious Examples

For newbies, good examples are devoid of abstractions. They are concrete and clearly—almost too clearly—convey the intentions of what we're teaching. They provide good *context*.

On the other hand, poor examples are littered with abstractions and vague differentiations. Here's a classic case of such an example.

When Clarity Met Sally

Imagine we're teaching a beginning programmer the basics of object-oriented programming. We might start, naturally, by discussing class constructors and object instantiation. At some point in our talk, we scribble a line of code like this:

```
Object myObject = new Object();
```

For us, this is a ho-hum line of example code. It says to create an instance of an object of type Object, called myObject. It's known to us that the name myObject is just any old name we decide to give this newly birthed instance. On the contrary, the constructor Object() isn't just named anything we want; it has to be named exactly the same as the name of the class.

We can mention all of this to our student. He can take notes and read them over again. To someone learning object instantiation for the first time, that seemingly straightforward line of code is going to look like this:

Object myObject = new **Object**();

For someone just beginning, it's hard to conceptualize which Object is the type, which is the constructor, and which is the name of the instance. Cover up that line of code and ask the student to rewrite it, and don't be surprised if he gives you something like Object Object() = new myObject; or my new Object = Object();.

Let's start making that example more obvious. Here's a better rewrite:

```
Object sally = new Object();
```

Now we're getting somewhere. Object is still important, but it's clear that it has no implications on the name of the instance of the object. It's also more evident now that the name of the instance lives to the right of its type.

Still, for a first-time object-oriented programmer, this could still be a little too in-the-weeds. Of all the possible types of objects we could create, the one called *Object* could very well be the most abstract of them all. Let's stick to our goal of avoiding unnecessary abstractions. Let's modify our example again, with a much more descriptive name:

```
Human sally = new Human();
```

Ah, yes! Now, Human is significant. The relationship between Human and sally is intuitive for anyone living on this planet, even for someone who doesn't write code for a living. It's obvious that sally is the name we've chosen to call this instance of Human.

However, something is still hard to understand. A newbie's next question might be this: if we already say "Human Sally," isn't it obvious that she's a new Human? What, exactly, is the point of a constructor?

Constructors that don't accept any parameters are fairly common in programming. For the seasoned developer, we're accustomed to working with classes that don't accept any parameters when instantiated. We leave them without parameters until we find good reason to add constructors that require more information at the time of construction. And so, the conventional new Object() (or new Human() or new List<DateTime>()) feels intuitive to us.

To the newbie, it seems mindless. Constructors that don't accept parameters and, even worse, don't do anything in their definition aside from instantiating the object, baffle the OOP neophyte. So, sometimes even the default approach to a concept isn't always the best example for teaching that concept to someone new. In this case, we're far better off making the example constructor accept a parameter (or two).

```
Human sally = new Human("female", 45);
```

Ask the newbie if he can create another human named Harry, who just got his driver's license, and there's a good chance he'll be able to figure out the answer.

```
Human harry = new Human("male", 16);
```

When showcasing examples, be overwhelmingly obvious. Sacrifice the default approach for the more explicit one. Cut out the generalities, generic names, and theory for something tangible and obvious. Even an example as fundamental as object instantiation went through four iterations to get to the point of clarity.

Essay 36

Lie to Simplify

When you teach something new, never start with the notion that everything you're going to say from here on out is 100 percent correct. Teaching a concept perfectly from the get-go is neither practical nor efficient. Any advanced concept is inherently difficult to understand. That's what makes it advanced. It's full of nuances, exceptions, and special cases that don't always fit into a nicely wrapped unified theory.

In contrast, when we learn something new, that nicely wrapped set of facts is exactly what we desperately crave. We want the hard and fast truths, whether or not they really exist, because they provide the foundation that helps us build our knowledge of any subject.

So, when you're the expert, let go of the intricate details of your domain at first. Let go of the "except when" and "but not if" cases; they just *aren't that important right now*. In the beginning, reveal the handful of rules that will get your student most of the way to understanding a concept well. Be comfortable with stretching the truth a bit to make the concept simpler. When you're teaching, white lies aren't always a bad thing.

When we pare down a complex topic into a less-than-perfect set of rules, it gives someone new a chance to build a solid foundation of understanding in their mind. When we teach subtleties and exceptions too early, before people have had a chance to soak in the general concepts, their learning becomes fragmented. Piecing together the whole story at once becomes difficult. It's hard to digest both rules and exceptions to those rules at the same time.

For instance, when I teach someone about the basics of database modeling, I always start with the notion that a good relational database needs to be strictly normalized without exception. By *Cheung's Law*, no two tables should carry redundant data.

In reality, there actually *is* a time and place to denormalize a database. For example, an *OLAP cube* is a type of database that breaks the conventional rule of database normalization in favor of redundant data.[1] Denormalized databases can make complex search queries much faster because they traverse fewer tables and require fewer relational JOINs. However, a novice shouldn't even care about that in the beginning until he's fully grasped the benefits of normalization. To understand the cracks in the foundation, he needs to intimately understand the foundation itself.

So, what if the understanding isn't 100 percent correct immediately? A solid foundation of understanding is motivating. And motivation will get them to an advanced level *faster*.

Essay 37

Encourage Autonomous Thought

As I touched upon in the previous essay, teach rules as if they were unbreakable laws of nature. It provides a structured starting point for a novice. To mature to an expert level, the training wheels need to erode at some point. Once the foundation has settled, the progressing student can start

---

1. http://en.wikipedia.org/wiki/OLAP_cube

deviating from the rules. Nix the training wheels, knee pads, and bike helmet.

The *Dreyfus model of skill acquisition* preaches this.[2] The Dreyfus model is, put simply, a model of how students learn. It was proposed in 1980 by a couple of PhD brothers (Stuart and Hubert Dreyfus) in their research at UC Berkeley.[3]

When we begin to master a subject like programming, we stop analyzing the rules to guide our work. That stuff just comes naturally. We start to think more abstractly. We envision multiple paths to achieve the same functional goal. There is no more recipe; there's just intuition. When our student starts finding that same intuition, we know we've done a good job. *Encourage that type of autonomous thought.*

How do you do that? After a while, you'll begin to see your student ask fewer and fewer technical questions in favor of strategy questions. That's the first sign they've mastered the "hows and whats" and are now looking for "why." When they start asking why, it usually means they think there's a better approach. What you've taught them is limiting their quickly forming natural intuition.

Keep *encouraging* that thought process. Don't suppress it with an iron fist. Get them to offer an alternative and go through the pros and cons. When there's a clear advantage to one approach, take the student all the way through the less optimal scenario so they see what pitfalls may lie ahead.

Down the road, the alternatives they give you will get even more compelling. At a certain point, you might even have them choose the path for themselves. There might even be a day when the student you've taught is now teaching you. That's not a sign you're losing a step; it's a sign you've really learned how to teach.

In this chapter, we looked at teaching from within: guiding our programming apprentices down the path of understanding what's in our heads.

---

2. http://en.wikipedia.org/wiki/Dreyfus_model_of_skill_acquisition
3. For a deep dive into the model, read Andy Hunt's book *Pragmatic Thinking and Learning* [Hun08].

But teaching our clients our ways has just as much merit too. In the next chapter, we'll talk about how teaching can foster a healthier relationship with the people handing you the paycheck.

CHAPTER 7

Clients

In this business, clients are our lifeline. Without them, what we do amounts to nothing more than a hobby.

However, quite often, the working relationship between us and them feels more like Ali vs. Frazier than Penn and Teller. In an ideal world, our client is giving us back rubs and feeding us scoops of vanilla ice cream, all while dabbing the corners of our mouths as we labor over their application. In an ideal world, our customer knows the agony we sometimes go through to fit nascent ideas into real code.

The harsh truth is simply this: clients rarely see what pains we go through to bend to changing requirements. Customers think only about that one new feature they want—the one that, in their eyes, involves "just changing this one little thing" when there's so much more to it. Stakeholders care only about the bottom line.

And that's OK. Like any relationship, the client-programmer relationship is a continual work in progress. It gets better when each side of the table understands what matters to the other. Working with clients *well* starts with understanding the view from their end so that we can start to teach them how things work from ours.

The Tough Client Is Ubiquitous

It's easy to start ranting about an awful client. But remember, this problem is not uniquely ours. In fact, we have it easy compared to some others.

When an architect designs a house, the homeowner sees only what's easily visible. She sees the obvious qualities of the home—the granite countertops, hardwood floors, and crown molding—not the subtle nature of a floor plan that the architect may have anguished over for months.

When a chef cooks a meal that's off by a salt grain, a picky critic delights in sending it back. The chef's work, completely nullified, is tossed away. I once saw a rather pretentious family's entire set of orders sent back to the kitchen because their teenage son lost his appetite over a hairy bug in his meal. The work of an entire staff of laboring cooks was thrown out because a customer mistook a fibrous piece of ginger for a cockroach.

We've all been the client at some point. Clients rarely appreciate the delicate, intricate, advanced thought that goes into the products they consume. And that is the cruel irony of it all. When I hire a plumber to fix the low water pressure in my shower, I simply want it fixed. I don't care if it's because of the main line, the flow constrictor, or a clogged shower head. A cheap bill and a revitalizing shower will do just fine, thank you.

In just the same way, when we build software for the consumer or client, the people we work with likely can't tell that we programmed the application with such elegance and cunningness.

What does this mean? No one we work for *cares* about our code, at least not immediately. It also means that, when they want to change our software, they haven't the slightest clue whether that change in code is easy, hard, impossible, or annoying. They don't know if their one *would-be-nice-to-have* request is really a *would-be-awful-to-build* one as well.

It's frustrating, yes. But don't pity yourself. You are not alone.

Demystify the Black Magic of Software

So, how can we get clients to appreciate our labors more?

Sometimes it starts with teaching clients *how* we do *what* we do. This is especially true when we're working with someone who has never had their own application built before. Even the most completely obvious things to us are not common knowledge to everyone else. I've learned this lesson many times in my career.

Years ago, I took on a freelance project for a client who wanted to build an online recommendation system. I was 22, a relative programming newcomer, and this project sounded like it had a simple objective. The application would offer the cheapest prices on bulk liquor purchases for bars and restaurants based on a database search.

Easy enough.

One weekend afternoon, we met over coffee to discuss the details. I assumed I would get a bunch of data in a neatly organized spreadsheet—a list of alcohol, brands, distributors, addresses, and costs. The user would request a particular bottle, hit a search button, and the app would go find the cheapest price in the system that fit the inputted search parameters. It all sounded peachy. My client and I agreed on the approach and went our merry ways. He'd consolidate the data, and I'd start building this rather *Simple, Elegant Example of Exquisitely Crafted Software*.

It took me about a week to get the foundation of the application built according to our initial meeting. A week later, we met for lunch to take a look at the Excel spreadsheet he had prepared. It looked a bit hairier than I was hoping for. It wasn't the simple five-column table I was expecting; I bit my lip and smiled sheepishly.

"Well, the prices change based on how much quantity of the product you buy," my client said. There were two other columns: a maximum and minimum quantity of alcohol that had to be purchased to obtain a specific price.

Fair enough, I thought. After all, that is the whole point of bulk purchasing. Back to the drawing board for a few slight tweaks to my data model and off we go.

The following day, I had the solution. I added a couple of additional fields, BeginRange and EndRange, to my database. I then modified the application so that it would accept a quantity value and adjusted the SQL query so the selection would filter those records where @quantity >= BeginRange and @quantity <= EndRange. The system was perfect again!

When we met the third time, my client looked puzzled. My code was beautiful, but there was something missing in the behavior of the system. As he played with the software, he noticed there were a few more levers missing.

As I would soon find out, in real life customers get discounts for coupling similar products together. The concept of bulk didn't just live per product, but buying X amount of whiskey might afford you a discount on Y amount of vermouth (Manhattan, anyone?). In addition, the discounts differed based on how much whiskey a customer purchased. Maybe we ought to throw in a few free jugs of Maraschino cherries as well.

From his end, the behavior of the system seemed off. In his experience, these deals, found by calling real human distributors directly, were commonplace. From my end, I didn't have the data or conditional logic to *deduce* any of this. In addition, even if he could get me all the data I would need, I'd still require a lot more time to figure out exactly how to organize it. Would I need to build some separate table of dependencies to handle discounted products based on the purchase of another product? Should I build a "common mixed drink" feature so the app could intuit what drinks a customer could make out of their purchases in order to offer other discounts? Most importantly, was there more madness to the model I would find out after this?

It dawned on me one day that I was not, in fact, building a concise, well-defined system to mine spreadsheets of data to harvest the singular right answer. Instead, I was building Larry^{TM}, the alcohol distribution manager. I was trying to account for decisions that were not easily deducible. Larry^{TM} gives offers based on his relationship to his customer, his own forty years of experience, and a general hunch or two. He knows what will drive customers back to his company as opposed to the other one hundred distributors he competes with.

Why wasn't I told all of this new information in the beginning? Was my client just hiding it from my prying ears, or did he not figure that it was important at the time?

Here, in full daylight, arose a fundamental misconception that lots of nontechies have about software. As programmers, we are primarily organizers of logic and information. Our jobs are mainly about pushing, pulling, manipulating, and displaying data. Most of us aren't in the business of artificial intelligence. We can't easily write programs that recommend or guess. Even "recommending" or "guessing" is a product of some set of defined, describable logic. Yet, sometimes, that's exactly how the outside world perceives this work: some kind of magic black box that can figure out all the loose ends even if we don't give it all the information it needs.

When I started to explain the difference between the software I was building with the software he was looking for, my client said he'd get back to me. Years later, my code is still sitting on an old laptop and is affectionately known as my *dust collector/paperweight*.

Looking back, the client-developer relationship became clearer to me. From my client's point of view, the Web, software, and databases—all these "technical" things—were all a mysterious haze of magic. There was some part of him that believed code could magically take care of a few undefined bits of logic, even if these small loose ends were the things that made this type of application really complex to build.

In any project, there will be a certain amount of unknown. This is the nature of our work. Rarely is an idea completely flushed out before we transition into development. Also, even when everyone thinks it is, it really isn't. Weirdness has a way of dodging our minds when we're still talking about software; it tends to surreptitiously unveil itself only when we start building.

Maybe that's why we build a love-hate relationship with our clients and customers. What is seemingly so obvious to those of us toiling "in the box" is sometimes lost to those on the outside, because it's in the box where the idea must finally be realized. It's in the box where we know, full well, whether we have something concrete or we don't. It's in the box where the real struggle occurs.

That's why there's frustration from the outside as well. From their vantage point, they've thrown you lots of information and requirements and detail—certainly enough to get you started. They let us know what they want, and they are waiting....

Further, when—days or weeks or months later—they see something that isn't quite what they had hoped for, they too are somewhat deflated. The box isn't as magical as they had thought.

When these times arise, take your client inside the box. Take them there early, if need be. Show them what you've been working on. Step them through the actual code if you must. Get them involved in thinking through the questions that naturally come up to you when you're in the midst of programming.

Essay 40

Define the Goals of Your Application

Working with clients isn't easy. The disconnect between you, programmer-designer-messiah, and them, unreasonable dictator-at-times, will always be there.

But not all clients are difficult. The better ones, the ones we want to keep for the entirety of our consulting careers, the ones we hope will always have new projects and new ideas ready to serve us at a moment's notice, all seem to have one thing in common.

Great clients put the *application* above themselves. When the application is the *most important part of the project*, everything else falls into place. Each feature decision can be scrutinized by simply asking the question, "Does this make the application better?" Feelings and personal objectives, both ours and the clients, aren't what dictate the outcome. When the product is not put at the forefront, clients will justify a feature request by other measures:

- "...it's something cool I saw on another site."
- "...because it's 1996, and everyone is using <blink> and a counter!"
- "...because it's 2005, and everyone is using RSS."
- "...because it's 2009, and everyone has a Facebook and Twitter badge."
- "...because my usability book told me that content below the fold never gets read!"
- "...because our CEO loves pink!"

At the beginning of the client relationship, establish the goals of the application. Decide, together, what the end product is hoping to achieve—and write it down. Doing this turns ammo like "cool" and "cutting-edge" into blank bullets. Establishing goals lets you say "no" with more conviction.

Essay 41

Be Enthusiastic and Opinionated

One of the biggest misconceptions nonprogrammers have with programming is that it's simply algorithmic. But we know it's not. Programming is as much art as it is science. We are passionate about our work in much the same way that artists are passionate about theirs.

It's our job to make that apparent. By doing so, we can change the relationship with our client. Development stops being just service work. We're no longer just the mechanics brought on to build the app.

Engage your client with the intricate details of your labor. Instead of simply giving them a couple of halfhearted options to solve their problem, offer them those same options with a strong conviction toward one. Then explain why. When a client sees your passion come through on even the most banal of options, they're more likely to give you the benefit of the doubt when your opinion differs from theirs. They'll view you as the *expert* in your own domain.

How do people in other industries make their work interesting to the consumer? It's easy to talk about Jamie Oliver, the "Naked Chef," who has popularized British cuisine, healthy eating, and generally mashing everything together with your hands. It's easy to talk about a musician like Jack White who, in Davis Guggenheim's rock guitar documentary *It Might Get Loud*, talks of his blood-stained guitars. It's interesting because cooking and music tickle the senses, and people will generally listen to famous people talk about their craft.

But let me vouch for some lesser known names.

Lou Manfredini is "Mr. Fix-It." He's an exuberant handyman who knows *everything* about fixing up a home. On his weekly Chicago radio show, he helps homeowners fix every type of problem. Whether it's installing a new HVAC unit, combating a leaky roof, or sealing a deck, Manfredini has a recommendation and opinion on everything. He's equally passionate about the type of paint you should use in your kid's room as he is about getting the vermin out of your basement.

Jeffrey Ruhalter is a fourth-generation master butcher in Manhattan. If butchering doesn't make you queasy, watch him butcher a pig[1] or trim a piece of dry-aged steak.[2] His eccentric style of communication oozes passion. He's someone whose recommendation you'd absolutely trust. You can't help but find his work *interesting* (unless porterhouse ain't your thing).

Manfredini and Ruhalter prove that you don't have to be in Hollywood to make your work interesting. They are heroes in otherwise unsexy vocations. We can do the same. Plus, I'd like to think programming merits more interest than leaky-sink fixing.

Essay 42

Be Forgiving and Personable

Passionate programmers have a penchant for being irritable. Providing the absolute last line of defense between nascent idea and functional reality can be frustrating. The entire thought chain prior to the code we write frequently lives in diagrams, functional specs, wireframes, and the brains of those who claim to be the "idea guys." Yet we're the ones faced with the daunting, often underappreciated task of transforming an idea into a real thing. Bugs live only in code, never in napkin drawings.

1. http://www.youtube.com/watch?v=kA7-KCBPvss
2. http://www.youtube.com/watch?v=rQiFEhsmOCk

In years past, software was this unapproachable, command-line-driven thing that only geeks, dorks, and nerds used. It was built by even geekier geeks, dorkier dorks, and nerdier nerds. Back then, it may have been OK to play the stereotypical role of the antisocial, generally off-putting curmudgeon.

Today, clients are everyday people, not just other software guys. They use the products of our labor like they use furniture. It's just there. The line between when someone is using software and when someone isn't is quite blurry. Technology is a mainstream industry now.

This means we need to button up how we work with the people we're building software for. So, when one of our clients, one who isn't tuned into how we work, asks whether they can just add another feature here that, in reality, breaks an already agreed upon assumption and undermines the entire architecture of your application, it's all too easy to quickly retaliate.

Instead, be forgiving. Understand the view from above the hood while you're entrenched working under it. If a client's request isn't practical, explain to them why. Give them an example scenario that opens up that "whole new bag of worms." Offer an alternative solution to solve the problem they're having.

In addition, make it a habit to talk to them in person. Hear their real voice and let them hear yours. Pick up the phone and call them instead of just emailing. You'll be surprised at how far a compassionate-sounding voice can go in getting things set your way.

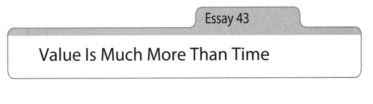

Essay 43

Value Is Much More Than Time

How much is our work worth to the client?

When we estimate the value of a project, it's pretty much industry-standard that we do so based on the sheer amount of *time* it takes. We take a guess at how long something might take, pad for uncertainties, multiply by an hourly rate, and hope the final estimate feels right to us before we push it to the client. There's an unsatisfying arbitrariness to it all.

Should working 200 hours cost twice as much as working 100 hours? Everyone, from individual contractors to multi-million-dollar development shops, has a billable hour.

Is this the way we should value our work? Does the amount of time we spend consulting, designing, developing, debugging, and testing really equate to how much value it's worth? I don't think it is. Unfortunately, it's the *only* metric that most of the world uses.

At many companies, time tracking becomes our individual value to the business. They mask it behind the ridiculously named concept of *employee utilization*. The more hours we can bill to a client, the better utilized we are.

But this completely discredits those moments that all programmers cherish when, in the midst of development, we suddenly come upon a more clever solution to a problem. In those lightning-strike moments of genius, we solve a problem in two hours that we initially estimated at eight. As an added bonus, we've done so in a way that's far more scalable than we originally imagined. Brilliant!

Wait, hold on a second. Put the champagne down. We now have to fill in those extra six hours with new client work, assuming it exists, lest our utilization numbers start tumbling down.

At companies like these, ones that look at programmer value as simply a scorecard of how many legitimate hours were spent fixing a problem, rather than other metrics that really equate to value, there's no incentive to think creatively. We're far better off toeing the line, working to fill in every hour we've been allotted, rather than dreaming up a more elegant solution. At companies like these, many programmers trade in their natural intuition to work more efficiently so they can legitimately get their utilization numbers up.

By simply basing cost on time, we equate the value of a piece of software (and the value of the service we provide our customer) with the time we spend building it.

In my opinion, those aren't the same metric. These two metrics have *very* different end goals.

The Value of Our Work Lies in Many Other Places

From a client's vantage point, many other metrics equal value. Here are just a few:

Flexibility

> Most clients—scratch that—*all clients* don't know exactly what they want up front. Be it features or font, clients need to see it on the screen to start figuring out what's working and what's not. The more we can adjust the course of our applications in midstream, the more value we provide. This is extraordinarily valuable to clients, especially those not so familiar with the medium.

Education

> When we work with clients, we're teaching them. They learn about the nuances of the Web (browsers, analytics, SEO, and so on) and the battles we face as programmers (How is this going to fit the data model? What makes a user experience a good one?). At the end of a project, they understand the medium much more than when they started. There's inherent value in that.

Personability

> When we're personable, friendly on the phone, and communicate eloquently, we're making a client feel good about who they've hired. That's value.

Expertise

> At my company, we drive the process in both how we work and which products we use. We have opinions. When clients come to us, they're often looking for us to provide the answers and recommendations. We provide value by being unabashedly firm about our opinions.

Speed and timeliness

> Shouldn't value also equate to speed? If we can build an app in half the time we proposed at the onset, why should we be compensated half as much?

Time as an Internal Metric

With so many other factors that impact value, where does time fit in? It's a critical metric but one that should track the internal health of the company or the individual contractor, not the value of the work. Time tracking answers these kinds of questions:

- Are we balancing the amount of work we're doing as a group and individually?

- Are there bottlenecks we can spot in our process that we need to fix?

- How much more can we take on while still maintaining the quality of our work?

Charging for a Product Rather Than a Service

So, if not time, then how do we measure the price tag we should put on a project and the services we provide for that project? How can we do so other than perhaps shifting the entire industry into a Wall Street–like marketplace, where the collective agrees that service X or product Y is worth this much today?

One method is to start turning your client work into a set of product offerings, much like you might sell a piece of software to an anonymous customer. If you're building something similar for a few clients (say, an administration tool to manage inquiries or a global search feature), you can start offering that component at a fixed fee for the next client. By productizing your client work, you can set the price to something you deem worthy of its value and then justify any future price hikes by those other value metrics.

At the same time, productizing client work keeps us honest. Suppose someone asks for a feature that we just built for another client. In theory, we wouldn't need all twenty hours we spent building that feature the first time. We'd probably need just a few of those hours to replicate it. Using time as the only metric, we'd only charge a fraction of the cost the second time around. But that makes no sense. That new feature has as much value for the second client as it did for the first.

Instead, if we use flexibility, expertise, and speed as metrics, charging the same amount the second time around *is* justified. We might even be able to improve on our first go-round and justify a higher price tag.

The value of our work is so much more than just the tick of the clock.

Essay 44

Respect Your Project Manager

If you're a developer who's worked with project managers before, I can say with 99 percent assurance that, at one time or another, you've been frustrated with them. While you're tackling a complex feature head on, here the PM is, with the nerve to ask you *when you think that might be finished*. While you've spent hours dissecting a deep, mission-critical problem in your code, here the PM is, nudging you to get that trivial button label fixed. And here the PM is again, asking you whether you can get that new client feature request that just came in out of the blue completed today.

You know the feeling. Deep inside of you, you believe the PM isn't doing much. He's simply asking you when, how, and if you can. You're the one sweating the details, doing the *real* labor, and earning your keep, right?

As developers, when our jobs get difficult, it's usually because there's a complex problem to solve in our software. We buckle down for a few hours and fight through the pain. We ebb and flow between spurts of frustration and ecstasy. For us developers, the hard work is in managing the product. We know everything about the application, and as discussed in Essay 40, *Define the Goals of Your Application*, on page 101, the application is what we should all be concentrating on.

Project Management Is Primarily People Management

But for a project manager, the goals are different. While good developers are the experts in the domain of the *application*, good project managers tend to be the experts in the domain of the *client*. They've developed an intimate working relationship with the guy on the other line or at the other end of the email. They know when they can push back or when there's something that's really important to the client—even if we might disagree. Client work can be an emotional struggle for the PM.

The Double-Edged Sword of Project Management

In a restaurant, it's the waiter who takes the heat for a soup too cold, a steak too raw, or an order too slow. If it's one of those particularly bad nights, the customer usually asks to see the restaurant manager to complain about "the worst meal they've ever had." As for the chefs in the kitchen? They tend to get off easy.

Yet, on those particularly good nights, the ones where a table has had the best meal of their lives, who gets thanked? Not the waiter. Not the restaurant manager. It's the *chefs*! Every now and then, they'll even come out for a bow.

It's the same story in our industry. From the client's point of view, the project manager *is* the company. In a team of other designers and developers, only project managers are the ones responsible for everyone else's actions. If one developer is pulling his weight but his fellow developer next door isn't hitting the mark, it's the project manager who usually has the lone, unenviable job of relaying the bad news to the client and then taking the heat.

But launch a beautiful app on time and on budget, and it's the developers who share in the praise. We're the ones who get the free pizza and beer lunches from a happy client.

Project management is important in ways that go beyond just the application, and it's oftentimes a thankless job. So, the next time one of your PMs asks you to implement a client's new feature request, don't immediately go whipping out your iron sword. Find out what's really driving the request. You might be able to recommend a simpler alternative. You could come up with a well-spoken argument against it altogether.

The more ammunition you can give a project manager to take back to a client, the more you empower them to do their job well.

In this chapter, we've seen the delicate nature of client management. In the end, good client management is often achieved through our own self-worth. When we're enthusiastic and engaging, clients get a vicarious taste of what makes this vocation great. When we're transparent and personable, a moment of potential conflict becomes a time to revisit the original goals of the application.

In the next chapter, let's get back to the nonhuman. There's an equally important relationship we must maintain between ourselves and our code.

CHAPTER 8

Code

Thus far, we've examined aspects of programmer life that have little to do with the very thing we get paid to do. This chapter takes us back home, to our roots, to the very thing we use to earn our keep.

Code is our essential material. But we typically don't think about code in the same way that any other builder thinks of their raw material.

Unlike any other kind of builder, we have an infinite supply of our material. Today we can distribute it to anyone, anywhere; distance plays no factor. We can replicate what we build at will. We can rapidly build upon and extend layers of code with more code. There's no time needed to let it dry or settle. No other medium in the real, physical world plays like ours does. And for those reasons, it's easy to take code for granted.

This chapter is about how we relate to code; it's an homage to the raw ingredient we use every day. I believe that the best programmers have a true *relationship* with code. They use code only when it's absolutely necessary, borrow code from others only when it's right, and even build their own frameworks with code when posed with the right challenge.

Essay 45

Write Code As a Last Resort

When residents of a New York City office building started complaining about the increasingly poor service of the elevators, the building management brought in a consulting firm to pinpoint the problem. The firm concluded that long wait times were the issue. Solving the tenant's complaints meant potentially adding new elevators and implementing new computer controls to improve elevator efficiency. These would be very costly adjustments.

Enter the young psychologist hired in the building's personnel department. He recommended, instead, placing mirrors in the elevator lobby. The problem wasn't waiting times; it was boredom.

His suggestion worked. People stopped complaining about waiting for the elevator when they had something to do: observe themselves in the mirror. The same problem was solved with a very different solution.

The most passionate of us are the ones who spend most of our work time thinking critically and creatively, often to find simpler, "lazier" solutions. The answer isn't always to plow ahead with the obvious, brute-force solution of writing more code.

Sometimes the best answers are found somewhere else. Ask yourself the following questions the next time you're confronted with a New York office building elevator problem:

- Has someone already done this task before? Can I use off-the-shelf code to take care of the dirty work for me?

- Is this piece of functionality really important to the goals of the application? Is the task already there but just through a different user experience?

- Is there a simpler way to code what I'm coding right now that might be worth the trade-off, even if it doesn't solve the problem entirely?

- Can I automate this task? Can I write software to write this algorithm for me so I don't have to repeat this work?

When we go straight into "writing code" mode at every task, we lose the opportunity to think about why we're really writing it. Instead, if we think critically about why we are writing code, we get to spend most of our programming time on the things that really matter.

Essay 46

A Plug-in Happy Culture

There's a beautiful irony to our medium. While scripting really *great* code is difficult, once we've written that exquisite code, we can redistribute it to the rest of the world easily, without any loss of fidelity or quality. Great code doesn't lose its intrinsic worth once a lot of other programmers have their hands on it. Quite the opposite, in fact.

As a community, programmers help out other programmers all the time. We can expedite many of our processes by pulling something off the shelf that our colleagues have built for us.

Building Apps Is Like Going to a Walmart

For instance, we can write more maintainable style sheets by using Sass before converting it to CSS. We have jQuery and CoffeeScript at our disposal; they are elegant frameworks that sit on top of JavaScript and hide all of its onerous syntactical nuances. Need a JavaScript plug-in to display images in a lightbox? There are at least thirty, written for *jQuery* specifically![1]

---

1. Thirty lightbox implementations: http://www.designyourway.net/blog/resources/30-efficient-jquery-lightbox-plugins/

Many younger developers have never had to write a raw SQL database query because object-relational mapping (ORM) tools and code generation frameworks do the tedious labor of transitioning data from a relational database to objects for us. Need an ORM tool? There are hundreds of open source and proprietary solutions.[2]

On the web application level, development frameworks like Rails and Django let us develop database-driven web apps while shielding us from most of the plumbing between the UI and database. Instead, we have the luxury of working within their softly cushioned walls.

For any task, large or small, on any level of the development stack, we can almost assuredly find a tool someone else has beautifully written to satisfy our needs. In most cases, it makes sense to use those tools. Even if they don't perfectly give us the functionality we want, even if we need to slightly bend our own preferences to conform to them, it's usually worth the time spared from building our own.

For instance, I'd never consider building my own continuous integration system. Jenkins (formerly Hudson) does it perfectly. I'd never, in a million years, write my own database syncing tool. I'll gladly spend a few hundred dollars on a tool like Red Gate than figure out all the edge cases involved in merging database schemas on my own. For most development tasks, I'll leave it to a piece of code written by people with much greater expertise in that domain.

To that end, building applications today feels a bit like going to a Walmart; maybe the open source movement is more like a Goodwill store. We can throw all these great toolsets into our cart, hit the checkout line, and go. Once we get home, we can unwrap all these great bits of code, stitch them together with a helping of our own, and give life to an application. We can get to running software *really, really* fast today.

The Backlash of a "Fast Code" Culture

Let's be thankful that using these tools doesn't cause the same public backlash as using "efficiency frameworks" in

---

2. See http://en.wikipedia.org/wiki/List_of_object-relational_mapping_software for a list of ORMs in multiple languages.

other industries. So long as our applications are designed and perform well, the material we use underneath goes unnoticed by the user. That's not a luxury that every industry has.

Take the food industry, for example. Back in the 1950s and 1960s, fast-food was hip. It was futuristic. It was progress. It fit the lifestyle of a nation that predominantly traveled by automobile and wanted a quick yet still satisfying way to enjoy food "on the go."

"Mmm! Just like Mom used to order!"

Yet a few decades later, those mystical magic food units began to fall out of favor. The quasi-automated nature of making such food has led to a major obesity epidemic in our society. Poor animal living conditions, hormones, and pesticides are, unfortunately, requirements to mass producing food at a low price. And besides all of those reasons, a culture simply fell back in love with *real, handcrafted food*.

Fortunately, we don't have that problem with "fast code." In other words, a renaissance in writing-every-bit-of-code-from-scratch-again seems unlikely. Leaning heavily on prebuilt libraries and frameworks to rapidly get applications up and running is very much here to stay.

But a backlash does loom. In each of these frameworks, much of the critical forethought has been extracted from us intentionally. What's left are very quick, high-level methods to solve otherwise complex problems. All those lightbulb moments of brilliance that their original creators discovered are now buried somewhere well beneath the programming interface.

With all the luxuries we have today with myriad efficiency platforms, we can quickly lose our appreciation, interest, and understanding for what's going on under the hood.

And that's a dangerous place to be.

Essay 47

Code Is the Ultimate Junior Developer

With the advantages we're afforded in our medium, it's quick to forget how remarkable code is.

For the time being, forget about the latest jQuery plug-in or Rails patch. Instead, imagine if the great mathematician, Carl Frederick Gauss, had the benefit of a programming language at his disposal back in the 18th century.

What Gauss Could've Done with Code

As a famous story goes, one day in grade school, Gauss's notoriously lazy teacher had the entire class sum all the integers from 1 to 100 in hopes of keeping the class occupied for a long while. Much to the teacher's chagrin, the young Gauss came back to his teacher after only a few moments with the right answer: 5,050.

How did he come up with the answer so quickly? If Gauss had the tools to program back then, he might have written some code like this to get to the answer:

```
public int sum_range_of_positive_integers_to_100()
{
    int sum;
```

```
for (int i = 1; i <= 100; i++)
{
  sum += i;
}

return sum;
}
```

After some quick thinking, he might have decided to rewrite his program more generically, in case the teacher was to challenge him again with a different range of numbers:

```
public int sum_range_of_integers(int first, int last)
{
  if (last < first)
  {
    throw new Exception("Last must be larger than first!");
  }

  int sum;

  for (int i = first; i <= last; i++)
  {
    sum += i;
  }

  return sum;
}
```

Of course, young Gauss didn't have such an option at the time. So, how did he get to the answer so quickly?

Rather than adding the numbers one at a time, he approached the problem in a far more clever way. Instead of summing the numbers linearly, he summed the remaining first and last numbers in the sequence instead, starting with 1 and 100, followed by 2 and 99, 3 and 98, and so forth.

```
(1 + 100) + (2 + 99) + ... + (49 + 52) + (50 + 51)
```

From here, a simple pattern emerges. It turns out there are 50 pairs of numbers that each sum up to the magic number, 101.

```
101 + 101 + 101 + ... + 101 + 101 + 101
```

The problem of summing all 100 numbers together was reduced to a simple multiplication equation:

```
50 * 101 = 5050
```

Gauss's approach was a uniquely human one. He took a problem that appeared tedious at the surface and came up with an elegant way to solve it. He found a better heuristic instead of resorting to the tedious linear approach that most of his classmates would've taken. As it turns out, he fell upon a nifty little formula:

```
The sum of all integers from 1 to n = n * (n+1) / 2
```

How would our code approach this problem? The code written earlier in this chapter would have produced the same answer, only doing it the "brute-force" way—the exact way we told it to do it. Given how fast processors work these days, software running our code would have arrived at the answer much faster than even Gauss did, despite the inefficiencies in its approach.

However, at a certain point, Gauss's approach would win out. If Gauss were asked to sum all the numbers from 1 to 4,000,000, sum_range_of_integers() would take a lot longer to compute.

This means that, at some number, Gauss would likely have been able to beat the code to the answer, because although the prodigy cunningly knew that the answer was to evaluate one simple formula, our poor program would've executed it this way:

```
1 + 2 + 3 + .... + 3,999,998 + 3,999,999 + 4,000,000
```

The Attractive Qualities of Code

Gauss's tale provides some interesting insight into how code solves problems differently from humans. Code thrives at the tedious stuff—at algorithmic, rules-based problem solving—far better than a human being. It doesn't just thrive; it has all the ingredients of an incomparably productive and affordable junior developer.

Code Doesn't Get Lazy

Code will never decide to just take a shortcut or find an easier way of doing things. The code snippet at the beginning of this chapter would sum up all 4,000,000 integers without deciding to just skip one. Code executes with impeccable precision.

Code Doesn't Get Bored

Imagine writing a small program like this:

```
int x = 0;

while (x != x + 1)
{
  // do nothing
}
```

As irrational as this task sounds, code will continue to crank at this nothingness forever, saved only by a runtime engine that would force an abort, sensing this loop would be going nowhere fast. Code doesn't analyze the importance of a task. It has no interest in its own well-being. It simply executes whatever we tell it to do.

Code Doesn't Forget

At the beginning of this chapter, we told the engine this:

> "Whenever I tell you to sum_range_of_integers(1,100), create an integer called sum. Starting with the number 1, add the value to sum, and then increment the value by 1. Keep doing this until you've hit 100. Then, give me back the value of sum."

Years later, I can go back to my program, call the method again, and expect the same result. Code doesn't forget what it's asked to do. Software systems, built upon thousands and thousands of lines of code, are equally adept. Code, no matter its volume, remembers what to do days, weeks, and years later. Could any human do the same?

Code Is Cheap

If a co-worker were asked to sit at his desk and sum all the numbers up from 1 to 4,000,000, we'd understand if he asked for money in return. Maybe we could work out some commission per summation agreement or agree to an hourly rate. Think back to Essay 8, *The Perks Are in the Work*, on page 20. For highly tedious tasks like this one, we're motivated by perks.

Fortunately, we've never taught code about money, market economies, or vacation homes. It performs for nothing in return. Once we've taught code something, we can take full advantage of it. There are no code-labor laws to get in our way.

Code Is Fast

Code executes at rates incomparable to the way we can finish tasks. It's metered by the limitations of hardware, which will become less and less limiting over time. Humans are absolutely no match for speed.

What does this all mean? Imagine a Craigslist ad that went like this:

Diligent Software Programmer Looking For Work!!! (Earth)

Teach me anything. I'll learn quickly and let you know if I need more information instantly. I will work whenever you want, however much you want. I will never forget anything you say and will never complain that I'm not being challenged. I am particularly good at tedious work.

- Location: Anywhere
- it's NOT ok to contact this poster with services or other commercial interests
- Compensation: $0

Code is inarguably the greatest junior developer who ever lived. It is uniquely adept at *tedious* yet *definable* tasks. It never complains—unless our instructions don't make sense. It's cheap, fast, diligent, consistent, and unemotional. Many companies would hire a dozen such programmers with these qualities in a heartbeat.

The power of code is extraordinary.

Essay 48

Separate Robot Work from Human Work

If code makes a dream candidate for a junior developer, then we ought to get it to work *right away*. The faster we can push tedious, algorithmic work off our plates—the kind of work perfectly suited to code—the quicker we can focus on the more interesting problems.

We have all had those moments of déjà-vu programming: pasting code from one project into another or wasting hours writing functionality we know we've written somewhere else before. On days that we're not inspired to rethink the entire process, we get through it and move on to the next task.

"Lately it seems like nothing but zeroes."

This kind of passive mentality has to stop. Instead of repeating even a small scripting task, we can write a program to do that work for us. A programmer's time is far too valuable to be wasted on repetitive tasks. When I co-founded We Are Mammoth in 2006, this is what I had rolling through my mind.

In the beginning, we built Flash applications with a .NET back end using C#. A few months into our business, I began smelling repeatable work: work that we were doing in the same mechanical way each time. Having seen the process for a few iterations, I started to separate the tedious yet algorithmic elements from the custom work that applied to each project we built. They separated like oil in water.

Every application we built followed a common set of conventions. After designing the database, we would write a series of stored procedures in SQL and then create objects in C# that would pull data from these stored procedures into their own properties. After that, we'd build a series of web hooks that would interface with another set of classes in ActionScript. Only then could we start developing any functionality on the Flash side. This hunk of development was tedious, banal stuff better fit for a *robot* than a human.

There were two components of an application that weren't algorithmic. The first was the database schema. We worked on applications for car companies, bed manufacturers, brokerage firms, software distributors, and fast-food chains. Their databases were custom-tailored to solving their own unique business problems. Second, we couldn't trivialize the user interface. They were custom-designed for each client. That's what we *wanted* to focus most of our time on.

This is when we stopped and took the time to roll our own code generator.

To better explain how we extracted the repeatable bits of our process, imagine building a blog from scratch. We'll start at the very bottom, with the database. The data model might contain three tables that look like this:

- Posts(ID, Title, CreateDate, Body, AuthorID)
- Authors(ID, FirstName, LastName)
- Comments(ID, Comment, Email, CreateDate, PostID)

If you're familiar with object-relational database modeling, this model is a fairly straightforward one. Posts has a title, a body, a create date, and a relationship to one Author via the foreign key AuthorID. AuthorID points to a record in the Author table by matching on the author's ID column. The Comments table contains a comment, an email address, a create date, and a related originating Post, via the foreign key PostID. The

PostID keys into the table Post by matching on the post's ID column.

Uncovering Repeatable Coding Tasks

In the early days of our business, we would start building an app by writing stored procedures to insert (i.e., create), read, update, and delete a record for each table in our data model. These "CRUD" methods were the base procedures for manipulating records in our database. Here's what I'd type to build an insert procedure for the Posts table:

```
CREATE PROCEDURE CreatePost (
  @Title NVARCHAR(255),
  @Body NTEXT,
  @CreateDate DATETIME,
  @AuthorID INT)
AS
INSERT INTO Post VALUES (
  @Title,
  @Body,
  @CreateDate,
  @AuthorID)
```

In the CreatePost procedure, we would simply take all the fields in the Posts table, besides the primary key (in this case, the ID field), and build a SQL INSERT statement with corresponding input parameters.

Because we can describe *exactly* how to write this kind of method by introspecting our database model, a program can *generate* any generic creation method. The same process described earlier could be repeated for the Authors and Comments tables.

We can apply this same kind of routine for generic UPDATE, READ, and DELETE procedures. For instance, to write an update procedure, we can take all the fields in a table and build a SQL UPDATE statement using the primary key fields (in our case, ID) as filters in the WHERE clause. Here is what the UpdatePost procedure would look like if we followed that prescription:

```
CREATE PROCEDURE UpdatePost (
  @ID INT,
  @Title NVARCHAR(255),
  @Body NTEXT,
  @CreateDate DATETIME,
```

```
  @AuthorID INT)
AS
UPDATE Post
SET
  Title = @Title,
  Body = @Body,
  CreateDate = @CreateDate,
  AuthorID = @AuthorID
WHERE
  ID = @ID
```

What other types of queries can we generate? For one, we can extrapolate selection queries based on the relationships between each of these tables. For instance, a post has an author. So, we could write a SELECT stored procedure to get all the blog posts by a specific author's ID. Let's call it GetAll-PostsByAuthorID. We could similarly write a procedure to get all comments by a post's ID (GetAllCommentsByPostID).

```
CREATE PROCEDURE GetAllPostsByAuthorID(@ID INT)
AS
SELECT * FROM Posts WHERE AuthorID = @ID

CREATE PROCEDURE GetAllCommentsByPostID(@ID INT)
AS
SELECT * FROM Comments WHERE PostID = @ID
```

Another formulaic pattern emerges in our stored procedures. For any foreign key [Y] in a table [X], we could write a stored procedure of the following form: GetAll[X]By[Y]ID.

Let's take it one step further. We might want to load records by filtering on a specific field. For instance, we'll need to get posts for a given day:

GetAllPostsWhereCreateDateEquals(CreateDateParam)

or authors by their last name:

GetAllAuthorsWhereLastNameEquals(LastNameParam)

Another formula emerges. For any filterable field [Z] in a table [X], given a parameter [P] we could write a stored procedure of the form GetAll[X]Where[Z]Equals([P]).

We can find similar tedious yet algorithmic processes when creating a C# data access layer, an API that our Flash layer would be able to consume, and the ActionScript layer itself. All that baseline underlying plumbing is fit work for the fictitious Craigslist job seeker we saw in the previous essay. Or, more realistically, we can *write smart programs to do the job for us*.

All of this would be a lot of work to do every time we started a new project. But by figuring out the *formula* for this type of work, we can relegate the *execution* of this type of work to...the robots.

Generating Code at Its Core

Taking the leap into code generation is an important pilgrimage every developer ought to take. It frees us to think about code as a powerful tool to transform how we work, not just as merely the material we use to write programs.

So, how do we actually write a generator? For a truly in-depth source, I highly recommend Jack Herrington's outstanding book, *Code Generation in Action* [Her03]. It covers detailed techniques and high-level patterns for generating code of all kinds. But we don't need that level of detail to get started. Here are the essentials.

Define Your Input Source

First, create an input source. It's the place that houses all the parameters our code generator needs to do its work. The input source can be as simple as a plain XML or JSON file or as robust as a database itself.

When we first deployed our company's code generator, X2O, we used an XML file as the input source. The XML file defined the tables, fields, and foreign keys for the database we generated code against. Here's an example of converting the blog data model in Essay 48, *Separate Robot Work from Human Work*, on page 120 into an XML input source:

```
<input_source>
  <table name="Posts">
    <field name="ID" type="int" identity="true" />
    <field name="Title" type="NVarChar" length="100"/>
```

```
    <field name="CreateDate" type="DateTime" />
    <field name="Body" type="NText" />
    <foreignkey name="AuthorID" to_table="Authors" />
  </table>
  <table name="Authors">
    <field name="ID" type="int" identity="true" />
    <field name="FirstName" type="NVarChar" length="50"/>
    <field name="LastName" type="NVarChar" length="50" />
  </table>
  <table name="Comments">
    <field name="ID" type="int" identity="true" />
    <field name="Comment" type="NText" />
    <field name="Email" type="NVarChar" length="100" />
    <field name="CreateDate" type="DateTime" />
    <foreignkey name="PostID" to_table="Posts" />
  </table>
</input_source>
```

Over time, your input source will grow. As you find more things to generate, you'll likely need more kinds of inputs. For example, a few months after building the first version of X2O, we wanted to augment our generator by having it create documentation. We added an attribute called friendly_description for each table and field node. We could then reference those attributes to generate API reference documentation for our ActionScript code.

Choose the Right Programming Language

Program in a language that's suitable for generating code. The language we write a code generator with doesn't have to be the same as the language the generated code is written in. In X2O, we use C# to write our code generators, but the output contains SQL, C#, HTML, and ActionScript.

The language of choice must have I/O capabilities so you can actually save the generated code output to your machine. Fortunately, pretty much any of today's popular programming languages (C, C++, C#, VB, Java, PHP, Python, Ruby, Perl) support this. If you've never read or written files using your programming language, spend an hour researching it. Your code generator will be doing a lot of this.

Herrington's preferred language is Ruby because of its I/O support and its support of text-template tools (like ERb and ERuby), and it plays well with XML, the input source language he uses in his examples.

Extract Your Input Source into Something Usable

With input source in hand, write a program to extract its contents into something usable. In our case, we mapped the contents of the XML file into its own object in C#. This lets you have both a system that's easy to work with when constructing the input source (XML) and a system that's easy to work with when you're generating code against the input source (like an object in C#).

In today's landscape, languages like E4X (ECMAScript for XML) make converting an input source into a programmatic object pretty seamless. Whatever method you use, it's critical to have an easy way to loop through and introspect your input source. You'll see why in the next step.

Combine Your Input Source Provider with Templates

With a usable programming environment and input source defined, the next step is to write templates. In our blog example, each tedious part of the development process had a formula. For example, to generate all CRUD statements, we do nothing more than loop through every table in our data model and apply the same statements for each. Take the SQL CREATE statements. We can take the following bit of real SQL code...

```
CREATE PROCEDURE CreatePost (
  @Title NVARCHAR(255),
  @CreateDate DATETIME,
  @Body NTEXT,
  @AuthorID INT)
AS
INSERT INTO Post VALUES (
  @Title,
  @CreateDate,
  @Body,
  @AuthorID)
```

...and replace the custom parts with replaceable variables...

```
CREATE PROCEDURE Create[cur_table] (
[List_of_attributes_as_input_params])
AS
INSERT INTO [cur_table] VALUES (
[List_of_attributes_as_SQL_insert_params])
```

...to create a template for generating CREATE statements.

With this template, we can loop through each table node in our input source provider and fill in the appropriate values. In this case, cur_table is just the name of each table, while List_of_attributes_as_input_params and List_of_attributes_as_SQL_insert_params are found by inspecting the field nodes of the input source provider.

In pseudocode, the creation of generated code looks like this:

1. Build an example file for the code you want to generate.

2. Create a template by extracting the custom parts and replacing them with variables.

3. Write code to read in the template file, loop through the input source, and replace the variables from the template file as necessary.

4. Write the newly created file to disk.

5. Do something with the files at the end (run them, compile them, and so on).

Component-Driven Design

A good rule of thumb is to keep all generators as separate libraries. Early on, X2O was a mass of code in one large file. The code that generated the database, SQL scripts, data access layer, web services, Flash objects, and CMS files all lived in the same library. While it worked, it grew to be unmanageable. It was harder to maintain because any minor change to the generator meant recompiling tens of thousands of lines of code.

Once we pulled each part out into about three dozen separate libraries, it was a lot easier to maintain. We could then chain all the generators together by referencing them in one all-encompassing master generator library. It also lets us toggle certain generators if we don't always need them.

Encapsulating and componentizing are good programmer habits anyway, but they're especially important when we're building dozens of little generators.

With these five simple tips in mind, we can get out of the starting gates.

Automate with Care

Is there anything *bad* about code generation? Are there times when we shouldn't be using it to our advantage? Yes. Here's a couple common mistakes you might make early on in your automation experience.

Avoid Touching Generated Code with Bare Hands

Make a strict rule that any generated code is not to be modified after it has been generated. Generated code is like fine china: you break it, you pay for it!

Generating code, only to go noodling around in it afterward, might make our process more tedious, not less. Why? Suppose we add a new field to our database and want to regenerate our new code against an updated data model. Each time we did that, we'd have to remind ourselves what we hand-modified and ensure the code is modified again.

If we really do need to noodle around our generated code, there are elegant ways around the problem. In C#, we can mark a class as partial. This lets us define a class in multiple source files. In X2O, every generated C# class is partial so that, if we ever needed to, we could add any additional methods or properties in a separate file marked with the same partial class.

If you don't have the option of partial classes in your language of choice, there are other elegant approaches too. For instance, you can extend classes or write custom helper classes.

Keep Generated Code as Tidy as Real Code

When we program by hand, keeping our code tidy is particularly important because we want it to be easy to maintain down the road. That's exactly why it's hard to motivate ourselves to keep generated code equally tidy—we never need to actually *maintain* the code we generate. We maintain only the generator.

That's why some argue that code generation is a trade-off between rapid output and custom-fit code—it creates a lot of excess that rarely gets used by the end application. Because it's so easy for programs to spit out code, we may not care as much to have it generate concise, optimized code. But this is something easily resolved.

Perhaps our next project doesn't need a certain set of data access methods. We can use our input source to define some optional parameters so that we're not spitting out sheets of excess code for a project that doesn't need it. As our generator matures, we might want to toggle certain code from generating. This is where component-driven design really helps.

Some argue that code generators produce inelegant code. However, this has nothing to do with code generators and everything to do with how we prescribe what our code generator should produce.

If our generated classes have duplicate functions or common methods, we can refactor the templates that make up our code generator. We can write the duplicate functions into a stand-alone class that lives outside the generator. We can still apply the same programming-by-hand techniques to our generated code.

In code generation, nothing stops us from still following good programming principles.

Know What Not to Generate

While code generation makes you think more critically about the patterns in your everyday work, it's equally important to not force those patterns. After the first few sweet victories of successful code generation, we might feel that air of invincibility and start trying to wrap everything into a code generator—even the things that really aren't automatable (but certainly tedious). It's easy to try to cram too much automation into things that are still too custom.

This is where we really have to consider the benefits of code generation. If our output code requires too many custom inputs to generate or requires too many hacks to use, we probably shouldn't be generating that bit in the first place. Just like bad code smells, there are also bad code generation smells.

Writing code generators gets us thinking about what is truly *automatable* and tedious vs. what is just tedious.

The Case for Rolling Your Own

Code generation and object-relational mappers are nothing new. When we built our own company framework in 2006, there were already plenty of comparable ones out there that we could've used. Certainly, it would have saved us countless hours of work in the beginning. Building any framework from scratch is a daunting task, especially when we know there are others that have been worked on for years.

So, in this plug-in happy culture, it begs the question, why would you ever roll your own framework, platform, or plug-in if there's something out there potentially just as good?

For me, there are three big reasons.

An Intimate Understanding of the Problem Space

When we're writing our own tool, we have no other choice but to completely immerse ourselves in the problems that the tool is desperately trying to solve. We must become experts in that domain. There's no going, "Well, I downloaded this library, copied this snippet of sample code, changed some of these parameters, and...I dunno, it just seemed to work." There are few things more unsettling than a programmer not knowing why something works but that it just works.

For example, many ORMs "lazy load" data by default, grabbing an object's relational data from the database only when it's been accessed in the object, instead of loading the relational data from the database up front. This is particularly efficient because the framework makes a database request only when we ask for it. There's less data stored in memory at any given moment.

For the novice ORM user, this might just be a nice-to-know type of thing. She might just keep programming against it without really concerning herself with the concept. In her test environment, the database has a sparse few test records, and the code she's writing against the ORM to pull back data is doing a dandy job. It just works.

But once she publishes her code to the live environment and real data starts to flow in, that seemingly benign little snippet of code she wrote using the ORM suddenly starts to bring the server to its knees. For example, an innocent piece of code like this...

```
foreach (Person person in myCompany.RelatedPeople)
{
  s.AppendLine(person.RelatedOffice.City);
}
```

...is actually making a database call for *every* person in that company to access his or her office location. That could mean thousands of executed queries in just a few lines of code.

When we're the ones building the tool, we have to know where all the potential gotchas live. When we're just the ones using other people's frameworks, we can let those gotchas slip past our radar until it's a little late.

Finding a Core Problem and Doing It Better

No matter what's available in the vast landscape of prebuilt tools, you can find a small sliver of something that can be done in a better way to fit how *you* program—to better conform to the types of apps *you* build.

In my case, the reasoning was simple. There wasn't a framework that would custom generate ActionScript objects that would directly tie into a database model. If I were to use something off the shelf, I'd likely have to use two distinct pieces of software: one to build up my .NET layer and a second to create ActionScript classes. If I ever made updates to my data model (which was often), I'd have to then rebuild these two disparate pieces of my application separately.

X2O is, in many ways, just like every other code generator, rapidly building objects that map to a database schema. But it is specific to the core needs of our business. No other tool generates code in the exact way X2O does. As our business grew over the first couple of years, we would tailor our software to our development workflow rather than let a piece of software we had no control over dictate how we worked. Building a code generator specific for database-driven Flash applications was the one fight we wanted to pick with what was out there. It was the problem we wanted to solve *better*.

The development team at Stack Overflow also went this route by writing their own micro-ORM. When they first released their programming forum site, they chose LINQ-2-SQL to handle all of their database queries. But as traffic and their data storage grew to a large enough proportion, there were noticeable performance leaks.

The way in which LINQ-2-SQL interprets a LINQ query, generates a mapped SQL query, and then executes that query was too inefficient given the amount of traffic they were supporting and how they were using the ORM. Queries were simply taking too long to execute on a traditional ORM.

Instead of swapping it for another off-the-shelf ORM, a couple of their lead engineers, Sam Saffron and Marc Gravell, wrote their own lightweight version called Dapper.[3] Dapper's execution is much faster because it does away with much of the overhead LINQ-2-SQL carries with transforming queries into relational objects. It accepts only raw SQL as input, circumventing some of the bottlenecks inherent to converting one domain language like LINQ into another like SQL.

However, what you gain in performance, you lose in robustness. Unlike most traditional ORMs, Dapper doesn't automatically map queries through to an object's relationships.

In the Stack Overflow code, Dapper was originally integrated in spots where there are performance bottlenecks, where losing some of the elegance of programming against a traditional ORM is worth the gain in execution speed. Now, almost all of their new work is done using Dapper. By rolling their own, Saffron and Gravell uncovered where the bottlenecks were and solved their specific problem *better*.

---

3.   Sam Saffron's piece on why they wrote Dapper: http://samsaffron.com/archive/2011/03/30/How+I+learned+to+stop+worrying+and+write+my+own+ORM

Programmer Hubris

Building our own toolset to do the work we do is the ultimate toast to our labors. What else could feel more satisfying to a developer than working on code that makes the future code we have to write that much easier? Building our own stuff is motivating.

When we're building our own toolsets, we learn a lot about what we value in our work. Oftentimes, these tools are the ones that *define* a career. Also, it's not just because they might help out other developers. They also uncover what we're hell-bent on improving. They cause the arguments we have a strong opinion about to bubble to the surface.

The tools we build are also *ours*. They're wrought with our own opinions about how something should be done. No one can tell us how we will build the tools that help us do our work. So, when we're writing our own little tools, we dictate what's important. For some, it's a nice escape from code we're writing for other people. This is where our pride as developers can shine through.

And pride is where we'll conclude our journey.

CHAPTER 9

Pride

The other day, I read an op-ed piece in the *New York Times* called "The Healing Power of Construction Work."[1] In it, a carpenter from Middle America talks about how an unusual number of his hired construction workers were also in trouble with the law at some point. Some of his best craftsmen were drug addicts and convicted felons. Even a paroled murderer was in the mix.

He wasn't suggesting that construction work attracted violent people. Instead, it provided some healing escape from their otherwise troubled lives.

There is a calmness when we work with our hands and a cerebral quality about using raw materials to build something. The carpenter's hired hands didn't treat construction work as merely a job. Rather, it was an escape from reality and a chance to do something really *well*.

Construction work has a primal reward to it: the satisfaction of creating something that didn't exist before. Construction is something that anyone physically able *can* do, if they learn, work hard, and care about the product. There's success to be gained, even for those who otherwise have not found it in other areas of their lives.

As I read the piece, it struck me that I approach programming in the same way. I am not a convicted felon nor do I personally know any fellow programmers who happen to be running from the law. Still, I do know many who believe,

---

1.   http://www.nytimes.com/2010/08/22/jobs/22pre.html

whether they'd like to admit it or not, coding can be a soothing escape from reality. Programming gives you that same joy of building something out of nothing.

Most programmers I know don't even care that much about *what* it is they build or who they're building it for. So long as they are solving an interesting problem and so long as there is an opportunity to build something elegantly, they are content. The exercise of dissecting a problem and solving it masterfully is the mental drug that keeps programmers addicted.

We build and design software because, whether found near the surface or buried deep into our souls, we actually *love* doing it. The best programmers I know toil over every small, sometimes insignificant, development decision. Like those construction workers, it isn't just about writing code; it's about writing code *well*.

Those who love this job aren't in it just for the money. There are easier ways to make money. This vocation is completely of our own choosing.

We Have a Marketing Problem

The problem? Few others outside our relatively small tribe realize how rewarding software development can be. Even many among us don't fully realize it. That's why I cringe when admitting I am a web-software-application-developer-guy. It all reeks of someone sufficiently intelligent just settling for something. Perhaps it has a lot to do with the nature of our work.

At our worst, we are disgruntled and unhappy, hopping from one job to the next. Our plight is no different from it is in any other industry. But the stigma comes because of how we exist when we're most passionate.

When we're really into our work, we live inside our heads far more than most. We stare at screens in a typing trance. We look out the window, seemingly longingly, when in reality we aren't seeing anything but pseudocode running through our heads. We aren't smiling or talking, and we seek no reciprocation. We simply want to be left alone, to our own thoughts, while the world does whatever it does around us. This is the passionate developer who's completely escaped the world around her.

When we are least excited, we are also quiet. We aren't smiling, and we don't want to talk with others. The only difference is, we type with less vigor and look out the window *noticing* the world around us and wanting to get out. When encouraged, we will in fact sigh, bang a fist, and mutter how much we disagree with the work we are doing. The disgruntled software developer looks just like the most fulfilled one, just with a noticeable sigh.

So, we have a *marketing problem*. The rest of the world sees programmers as a breed of recluse headphone geeks rather than what we really are: passionate craftspeople and thinkers. Why is this?

Lessons from the Cooking Industry

Take the cooking industry. Emeril Lagasse, Bobby Flay, Mario Batali, and Gordon Ramsay are exuberant (sometimes annoyingly so) chefs whose passion oozes from their pores. Their passion reaches not just other chefs but the *masses*. Our (less famous) contemporaries don't have that same kind of global appeal. There are no programmer celebrities whose reach stretches beyond the engaged eyes of their fellow programmers.

At first, you may think it's because people generally want to cook more than they want to program. However, I can assure you that while I routinely salivate when a chef prepares a *horseradish-crusted salmon with braised greens and smashed new potatoes*, I will not be making one for myself anytime soon. The cooking industry has found a way to sell its craft to everyone, even if many of us will never deglaze a pan in our lives.

Maybe it's because we just like to eat. Food is visually stimulating. Watching someone prepare a meal stirs our most primal emotions. Some call it *food porn*. But the modern-day buzz about food hasn't always been like this. After all, cooking shows have been around for decades. Most of us have heard of Julia Child, but ever hear of Justin Wilson, Jeff Smith, or Graham Kerr? They had their own cooking shows for years but lived in a far less cooking-crazed society. They never gained the omnipresent appeal their modern-day contemporaries have today. What shifted?

In the olden days, cooking shows felt like being in your grandmother's kitchen. A couple of cameras and some pedantic talk about a quarter cup of this and a teaspoon of that. Cooking shows were made for people who wanted to...*cook*. They never stretched further beyond their audience. Cooking was just about cooking. Today's shows slice from a completely different angle.

First, they emphasize the detail. There's the close-up shot, and then there's the closer-up shot—the one where you can see the marbling of a thick slab of tenderloin while double-checking that the chef's fingernails are clean. HD television has helped the food industry, as much as any other industry, sell its stuff. In bygone days, a steak was just a steak. Now, it's about the intricate marbling, flowing juices, and grill marks. The *detail* is where the appeal lives.

Second, today's shows make cooking approachable to everyone. Long gone are the days where TV cooking was just about following a recipe. Today's shows emphasize simplicity. Everyone can do it. Thirty-minute meals, $5 dishes, and having a good time with friends. Cooking is feasible and entertaining.

Chefs play up their food like royalty. Passion lives in their description of ingredients and flavors, even if only using nondescript adjectives like *fresh*, *flavorful*, and *zesty*. Nowadays, chefs always taste their own food (usually at the climactic end of the show), exalting what magic it's doing to their taste buds in sensationalized "mmms."

Even further, *the bad stuff sells*. Go to a real restaurant kitchen on a Friday night and see the real story. Screaming, sweat, dropped food, and a general disaster waiting to happen. "System D" in Anthony Bourdain's *The Nasty Bits* tells a far different story from the pristine world of cooking that's sometimes portrayed on television, and it's a *New York Times* best seller.

On TV, Gordon Ramsay has made infamous the state of affairs at many restaurants on their deathbeds. *Kitchen*

Nightmares is the raw truth about how poorly a restaurant can operate and still run. Watching a restaurant pull itself out of near-certain catastrophe is, apparently, *entertaining*. The cooking industry has learned how to sell their commodity to the masses.

Other industry leaders have found the magic elixir as well. They present their craft in a way that tickles our senses enough to make someone who has no real interest in their craft care about it.

Don't agree? Just flip through your television on a weeknight. Over the past few years, in the United States and Europe, there have been wildly popular shows on crab catching (*Deadliest Catch*), dog training (*The Dog Whisperer*), children's choirs (*The Choir*), dieting (*The Biggest Loser*), babysitting (*Supernanny*), blue-collar dirty jobs (*Dirty Jobs*), and raising octuplets (*Jon and Kate Plus 8*). These aren't exactly glamour industries.

"A girl, a hunky bachelor, and seven dwarves?!
You *sure* this isn't a reality show?!"

Then, why not software development? Why can't we be among those who have figured out what makes their line of business marketable? Code lets us play games, make friends, converse with them from anywhere on this planet, find love, buy anything, monitor the sick, organize our lives, and do everything in between. We create these magical tools *every day.* We have a captivating story to tell. Just ask the guy over there who's not saying a thing.

I'm not suggesting *Top Programmer* or *Coding Nightmares* are in pilot production anytime soon. But we ought to put ourselves out there with the masses. We build the tools that run today's society, and every day, there are those among us figuring out how to build them faster, cheaper, and more beautifully than ever before. Programming is a fascinating job. It's up to us to show the rest of the world.

The software world is, at its best, a beautifully run kitchen. At its worst, it's a complete organizational nightmare. *Legacy* usually means something grand and eternal in every other context besides what it means in software. We also live in a constantly changing medium. What we're using today will seem archaic five years from now. These are all viable topics for the masses.

We need to do it in small steps. It starts with the way each of us treats our work. At restaurants, good waiters take pride in presenting a dish. It's not just the chef's dish; it's the waiter's dish too. The craft of it distinguishes mere sustenance from exquisite cuisine. In the same sense, we ought to take pride in our work. Let's take off the headphones more often and talk to as many nontechies as we can. Software development has a great story to share.

The process of building software can be interesting and entertaining. What we do *is* a marketable business. It's up to us to make it more than just about code, just as the cooking world has made their work more than just about ingredients. Let's disseminate it to others with passion.

It's a struggle I have every day. Whenever I'm asked what I do for a living, I shrug.

I want to say that I'm a web developer and designer—a modern-day programmer, if you will. However, "programmer" just doesn't have the ring I'm looking for. It lacks the chutzpah of doctor, architect, or President of the United States. "Doctor" means miracle worker, "architect" alludes to the dreamer and master builder, and I hear being President has a few perks as well.

To the layperson, programmer equates to "working with computers," which carries about as much validity as equating a surgeon to "working with sharp things." The next time someone asks me what I do for a living, I'll tell them I'm a country music star. It's just easier.

We are, in fact, sometimes doctors, architects, and rulers all at once. We work miracles with our code, dream, build, and lay down the law. This is the book I will give them when they ask me what I do.

Bibliography

[CB06]   Ka Wai Cheung and Craig Bryant. *Flash Application Design Solutions: The Flash Usability Handbook*. Apress, New York City, NY, 2006.

[FH10]   Jason Fried and David Heinemeier Hansson. *Rework*. Crown Business, New York, NY, 2010.

[Gol05]   Natalie Goldberg. *Writing Down the Bones: Freeing the Writer Within*. Shambhala Publications, Boston, MA, 2005.

[HH07]   Chip Heath and Dan Heath. *Made to Stick: Why Some Ideas Survive and Others Die*. Random House, New York, NY, USA, 2007.

[Her03]   Jack D. Herrington. *Code Generation in Action*. Manning Publications Co., Greenwich, CT, 2003.

[Hun08]   Andrew Hunt. *Pragmatic Thinking and Learning: Refactor Your Wetware*. The Pragmatic Bookshelf, Raleigh, NC and Dallas, TX, 2008.

[Ker04]   Joshua Kerievsky. *Refactoring to Patterns*. Addison-Wesley, Reading, MA, 2004.

[Pin09]   Daniel H. Pink. *Drive: The Surprising Truth About What Motivates Us*. Riverhead Books, New York, NY, USA, 2009.

Learn to Program

Learning to program for the first time? Here's how to do it Ruby or Python.

For this new edition of the best-selling *Learn to Program*, Chris Pine has taken a good thing and made it even better. First, he used the feedback from hundreds of reader e-mails to update the content and make it even clearer. Second, he updated the examples in the book to use the latest stable version of Ruby, and also to use code that looks more like real-world Ruby code, so that people who have just learned to program will be more familiar with common Ruby techniques.

Chris Pine
(240 pages) ISBN: 9781934356364.
$24.95
http://pragprog.com/titles/ltp2

Welcome to computer science in the 21st century. Did you ever wonder how computers represent DNA? How they can download a web page containing population data and analyze it to spot trends? Or how they can change the colors in a color photograph? If so, this book is for you. By the time you're done, you'll know how to do all of that and a lot more. And Python makes it easy and fun.

Jennifer Campbell, Paul Gries, Jason Montojo, Greg Wilson
(350 pages) ISBN: 9781934356272.
$32.95
http://pragprog.com/titles/gwpy

Think Better

Want to concentrate more effectively, and learn how to take advantage of your brain's wiring? We've got you covered.

Do you ever look at the clock and wonder where the day went? You spent all this time at work and didn't come close to getting everything done. Tomorrow, try something new. Use the Pomodoro Technique, originally developed by Francesco Cirillo, to work in focused sprints throughout the day. In *Pomodoro Technique Illustrated*, Staffan Nöteberg shows you how to organize your work to accomplish more in less time. There's no need for expensive software or fancy planners. You can get started with nothing more than a piece of paper, a pencil, and a kitchen timer.

Staffan Nöteberg
(144 pages) ISBN: 9781934356500.
$24.95
http://pragprog.com/titles/snfocus

Software development happens in your head. Not in an editor, IDE, or design tool. You're well educated on how to work with software and hardware, but what about *wetware*—our own brains? Learning new skills and new technology is critical to your career, and it's all in your head.

In this book by Andy Hunt, you'll learn how our brains are wired, and how to take advantage of your brain's architecture. You'll learn new tricks and tips to learn more, faster, and retain more of what you learn.

You need a pragmatic approach to thinking and learning. You need to *Refactor Your Wetware.*

Andy Hunt
(288 pages) ISBN: 9781934356050.
$34.95
http://pragprog.com/titles/ahptl

Feel the Power

The command line remains the ultimate power tool for developers, and now your Ruby apps can take full advantage of this environment. And while we're tweaking environments, how about starting with your Mac?

Speak directly to your system. With its simple commands, flags, and parameters, a well-formed command-line application is the quickest way to automate a backup, a build, or a deployment and simplify your life.

David Bryant Copeland
(200 pages) ISBN: 9781934356913. $33
http://pragprog.com/titles/dccar

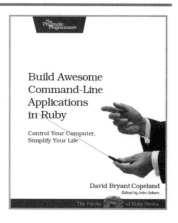

Exploit secret settings and hidden apps, push built-in tools to the limit, radically personalize your Mac experience and tweak your system so it's just right for you. Every one of these 300 quick and easy tips, tricks, hints and hacks in *Mac Kung Fu* makes "it just works" even better. Become the ultimate Mac user, working faster, smarter, and simply have lots more fun with your Apple computer.

Keir Thomas
(320 pages) ISBN: 9781934356821. $35
http://pragprog.com/titles/ktmack

Be Agile

Don't just "do" agile; you want to *be* agile. We'll show you how.

The best agile book isn't a book: *Agile in a Flash* is a unique deck of index cards that fit neatly in your pocket. You can tape them to the wall. Spread them out on your project table. Get stains on them over lunch. These cards are meant to be used, not just read.

Jeff Langr and Tim Ottinger
(110 pages) ISBN: 9781934356715. $15
http://pragprog.com/titles/olag

Here are three simple truths about software development:

1. You can't gather all the requirements up front. 2. The requirements you do gather will change. 3. There is always more to do than time and money will allow.

Those are the facts of life. But you can deal with those facts (and more) by becoming a fierce software-delivery professional, capable of dispatching the most dire of software projects and the toughest delivery schedules with ease and grace.

Jonathan Rasmusson
(280 pages) ISBN: 9781934356586.
$34.95
http://pragprog.com/titles/jtrap

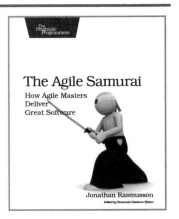

Career++

Ready to kick your career up to the next level? Start by growing a significant online presence, and then reinvigorate your job itself.

Technical Blogging is the first book to specifically teach programmers, technical people, and technically-oriented entrepreneurs how to become successful bloggers. There is no magic to successful blogging; with this book you'll learn the techniques to attract and keep a large audience of loyal, regular readers and leverage this popularity to achieve your goals.

Antonio Cangiano
(250 pages) ISBN: 9781934356883. $33
http://pragprog.com/titles/actb

This book is about creating a remarkable career in software development. In most cases, remarkable careers don't come by chance. They require thought, intention, action, and a willingness to change course when you've made mistakes. Most of us have been stumbling around letting our careers take us where they may. It's time to take control. This revised and updated second edition lays out a strategy for planning and creating a radically successful life in software development.

Chad Fowler
(232 pages) ISBN: 9781934356340.
$23.95
http://pragprog.com/titles/cfcar2

The Pragmatic Bookshelf

The Pragmatic Bookshelf features books written by developers for developers. The titles continue the well-known Pragmatic Programmer style and continue to garner awards and rave reviews. As development gets more and more difficult, the Pragmatic Programmers will be there with more titles and products to help you stay on top of your game.

Visit Us Online

This Book's Home Page
http://pragprog.com/titles/kcdc
Source code from this book, errata, and other resources. Come give us feedback, too!

Register for Updates
http://pragprog.com/updates
Be notified when updates and new books become available.

Join the Community
http://pragprog.com/community
Read our weblogs, join our online discussions, participate in our mailing list, interact with our wiki, and benefit from the experience of other Pragmatic Programmers.

New and Noteworthy
http://pragprog.com/news
Check out the latest pragmatic developments, new titles and other offerings.

Save on the eBook

Save on the eBook versions of this title. Owning the paper version of this book entitles you to purchase the electronic versions at a terrific discount.

PDFs are great for carrying around on your laptop—they are hyperlinked, have color, and are fully searchable. Most titles are also available for the iPhone and iPod touch, Amazon Kindle, and other popular e-book readers.

Buy now at *http://pragprog.com/coupon*

Contact Us

Online Orders:	*http://pragprog.com/catalog*
Customer Service:	*support@pragprog.com*
International Rights:	*translations@pragprog.com*
Academic Use:	*academic@pragprog.com*
Write for Us:	*http://pragprog.com/write-for-us*
Or Call:	+1 800-699-7764